ARABS UNSEEN

Dear Rohit,

(hope it's not like reading about
those fine young
Arabs ..

[signature]

Rahaan
Paris 2017

ARABS UNSEEN

MOHAMMED MAHFOODH ALARDHI

BLOOMSBURY
NEW DELHI • LONDON • OXFORD • NEW YORK • SYDNEY

Contents

Introduction	1
Joumana al Jabri and Ramzi Jaber: A Laboratory for Change	11
Lotfi Maktouf: Almadanya	23
Mohammed Saeed Harib: Freej	35
Mutassem al-Sharji: The Enriching Experience	46
Raghda El-Ebrashi: Alashanek Ya Balady	57
Safiya al-Bahlani: An Artist's Evolution	69
Sarah Hermez: Creative Space Beirut	80
Soraya Salti: Injaz al-Arab	91
Sultan Batterjee: A Developer with a Cause	103
Tariq al-Barwani: Knowledge Oman	114
Conclusion	126

Introduction

FROM A VERY YOUNG AGE, I KNEW I WANTED TO FLY.

In the evenings, lying on my bed, I would imagine myself in the cockpit, a professional pilot alone before an instrument panel of innumerable knobs and dials, running through the pre-flight routine.

Hydraulic pressure? Okay. Flight controls? Unlocked. Emergency Warnings? None... Full power? On...

And then away I would go, fleeing reality for a few brief minutes of freedom in the skies, soaring over the windswept sands of the Empty Quarter, the great *Rub' al Khali*, or swooping and diving, birdlike, above the boundless blue of the Indian Ocean. There was nowhere I couldn't go, no limit to the heights I could climb, and as the world fell away below my wings, the city disappearing from view, I felt what could only be described as pure joy.

Eventually, of course, the dream would end, and reality would be there waiting for me when I returned. Although it was always a very vivid dream, my heart racing as fast as the plane would fly, the wind whistling over the wings, I never imagined that such a thing could one day come true.

After all, the Oman of my childhood was a far different place, a far *poorer* place, than the one I live in today. The idea that I might grow up to *be* something, to achieve in life, had never occurred to me. For that, Oman was not a country that invested in its people. On the contrary, it kept them in the dark, in a Middle Ages of its own making, a hidebound society hermetically sealed off from the rest of the world.

There was practically nothing then: no running water, no electricity, and no national infrastructure of any kind. Radios were banned, as were newspapers and even the eyeglasses a person might need to read one. Though, of course, few could; the vast majority of Omanis were still illiterate. In a population of 750,000 people, fewer than a thousand pupils were enrolled in school – all of them boys and all in primary grades.

Equally scarce was anything resembling modern health care. With only five hospitals in the entire country, and just a few dozen beds between them, most people still relied on traditional healers. To get to them, or anywhere else, they rode camels or donkeys – or they walked, mile after mile, in the withering heat. The only cars in the country belonged to the Sultan and the handful of people granted licenses to purchase their own. But with just 6 miles of paved road – a single strip stretching from the royal palace to the airport – there was nowhere to drive anyway.

Thus, at the dawn of the information age, when the blueprint for the Internet was first emerging, when the first satellites were orbiting the Earth, and the first lasers were flashing to life, Oman was still an island unto itself, frozen in time and forgotten by progress. It wasn't until 1970, the year I turned 9, that His Majesty Sultan Qaboos bin Said replaced his father on the throne, paving the way for a nationwide modernisation that continues to this day; a period we refer to as the Renaissance.

Of course, it wasn't always this way. Oman has a proud heritage. The oldest independent state in the Arab world, it was long the link between East and West, Africa and Arabia. Muscat, the country's fabled port city and present-day capital, had for centuries been a cosmopolitan centre of commerce, the seat of a sprawling maritime empire. With its strategic location on the southeastern tip of the Arabian Peninsula, Oman held sway over the Indian Ocean, dominating the lucrative trade routes from the Moorish Spain to the South China Sea. At its peak in the 17th century, Omani influence extended throughout the Persian Gulf, as far east as India, and as far south as Zanzibar.

Meanwhile, Oman itself became a meeting ground for people of myriad faiths and cultures. While Omani vessels were sailing into distant harbours, Omani seaports served as a magnet for foreign merchants. Chinese, Indian, Dutch, Portuguese and Persian: those and others rode the monsoon winds to Muscat, bringing with them the riches of faraway civilisations: gold and pearls from the Persian port of Basra, coffee, tea, and spices from southern India, coral and ivory from the Kenyan coast, and a great deal more.

That seafaring tradition fostered a culture of tolerance and openness, for which Omanis are known today. Though Islam is the country's official faith, Christians, Hindus, Buddhists and Baha'i have long called Oman home, and their places of worship can be found throughout the country. Indeed, long before it was written into law, religious freedom was a fundamental feature of Omani society, the manifestation of a worldview informed by centuries of overseas commerce and colonisation.

Eventually, Oman's empire would collapse, as the economy faltered and the Sultanate's power declined. But the people of Oman never lost their sense of the world beyond its borders. Even as the country descended into darkness, isolated from any outside influence, and untouched by progress, they held onto the hope that someday things would change. That day came on July 23, 1970, when His Majesty Sultan Qaboos bin Said assumed power.

In the four decades since, Oman has made enormous strides. In fact, according to the United Nations, no country has come further over the past 40 years; in 2010, the U.N's Human Development Index, which compares countries on measures of life expectancy, education and relative income, listed Oman at the top of the world's 10 leading countries in terms of improvement.

That improvement began immediately. No sooner had His Majesty assumed power, he lifted his father's harshest restrictions on personal freedom – bans against singing and smoking, listening to the radio, and dressing in European clothes. Within a few short years, he had embarked on an oil-fuelled construction boom that saw the rise of new office buildings, a modern airport, new schools, and hospitals and hundreds of miles of asphalt highway. By 1985, 145,000 girls and boys were enrolled in some 475 schools.

As Oman grew up, so did I. Born in the ancient city of Sur, I was 8 years-old when my father, a customs official, was transferred to Al-Aswad, a small city near the border with the United Arab Emirates. It was a desolate patch of desert, but not far from our house was a small airstrip, where, every so often, a military aircraft would arrive with supplies for the army. To a boy who had only seldom glimpsed a car, and never once watched a television, those planes were a sight to behold. The moment I heard the buzz of engines in the sky, I would sprint to the tarmac and sit there mesmerised as the aircraft approached, landing right before my eyes.

If someone had told me as that young boy that I would grow up to be a pilot myself; that I would fly fighter jets in Oman's Royal Air Force, and that I would one day rise to the rank of Commander, I would never have believed it. It's a testament to Oman's progress under His Majesty, to its emergence as a model modern Arab state, and one that counts its wealth not in barrels of oil but in educated minds that this is precisely what happened.

This book is, in part, homage to that remarkable feat – to the triumph of human industry and will that is my native Oman. But it is primarily an attempt to instill in readers that same sense of pride in the Arab society as a whole by shining a light on change agents throughout the region. Just as our Sultan, by his vision and leadership, has made Oman what it is today, innovators across the Arab world are forging new paths, rethinking the status quo, and daring to do things differently. Together, they are writing a new chapter in the region's unfolding transformation.

To be sure, the Arab world is now at a watershed. With some 220 million people under the age of 30, it has the world's second highest percentage of youth, trailing only sub-Saharan Africa. The region also has one of the highest rates of joblessness; approximately 10 per cent of the population is unemployed. Young people shoulder a disproportionate share of that burden, and as more and more enter the job market, the need to absorb them grows more urgent.

According to the World Economic Forum, MENA countries will have to create some 75 million jobs by 2020, just to maintain employment at current levels. How leaders address this challenge will determine whether those youth drive future growth and prosperity or hinder economic development, potentially inflaming the unrest that has gripped the region in the wake of the Arab Spring uprisings.

As the experience of Oman shows, one key to avoiding the latter is promoting education for all. Whereas in 1970, there were only three schools in the entire country, Oman today has more than 1,200, guarantees free education through high school for boys and girls alike, and boasts a range of public and private universities. It's upon this educational foundation that His Majesty built the modern state we have today. As Oman transitions to a knowledge-based economy, education reform with an emphasis on critical thinking and life skills remains a national priority.

Of course, education alone does not create jobs. If Oman and other MENA countries are to achieve that transition, and to successfully address the challenge of youth unemployment, it's imperative that we – business leaders, policy makers, educators – cultivate a climate of innovation, one in which business can flourish and entrepreneurs can thrive. Meanwhile, we have to foster in young people the conviction that they themselves can be the engines of change. That, as entrepreneurs, they can generate ideas, launch new ventures, and create the jobs the region so urgently needs.

For the youth of the Arab world, entrepreneurship offers the promise of empowerment. But entrepreneurs will only emerge from an education system that nurtures their talents and provides them with the knowledge and skills they need to succeed. As it is, entrepreneurs in the Arab world are severely underserved, with little access to formal education or qualified instructors. According to a recent report by the World Economic Forum, fewer than 10 percent of universities in the MENA region offer courses on entrepreneurship and just five universities offer a major in the subject.

But there are signs of change. Universities in Saudi Arabia are beginning to strengthen ties with the country's business community through initiatives like the Innovative Industrial Collaboration Program at King Abdullah University of Science & Technology (KAUST). At Abu Dhabi University in the United Arab Emirates, the Centre of Innovation and Entrepreneurship is bridging the gap between academia and industry by helping students incubate their start-ups. Also, in countries across the region, an organisation called Injaz al-Arab is sending thousands of private-sector volunteers into schools to teach kids financial literacy and the basics of starting a business.

Slowly but surely, this movement is gaining strength, and yet, amid the region's upheaval, much of the good news is going unnoticed.

One reason for this is the news media's tendency to portray Arab youths not as budding entrepreneurs but as criminals and terrorists, an image that belies their immense power to affect positive change. Drowned out by unrelenting reports of bombings, kidnappings, and executions, by the daily horrors of war, are quieter stories of success. These stories challenge the prevailing stereotypes, and as a result, seldom make headlines. But they are no less relevant to the world around us, and no less worthy of our attention.

No, in fact, they demand it. For far too long, we have looked to our past for inspiration – for examples of greatness from the Golden Age of Islam, and to be sure, we have much to be proud of; the Arab world has nurtured a number of brilliant minds, men, and women, whose contributions – to mathematics and medicine, physics and biology, poetry and philosophy and much more – shaped the course of history and are deeply cherished around the world.

Take, for example, Ibn al-Haytham, the 11th century scientist, polymath, mathematician and philosopher from Basra. Known throughout Europe simply as 'The Physicist', al-Haytham is regarded by many as 'the first true scientist' for his pioneering work on the scientific method. His scholarly interests ranged widely, and his discoveries in everything, from celestial physics to visual perception, strongly influenced the work of later scientists in the West, including the likes of Robert Bacon, Leonardo da Vinci, and Galileo.

Medicine benefitted enormously from the work of the eminent Arab physician Ibn Al Nafis. Born in 13th century Damascus, Al-Nafis was the first to accurately describe pulmonary circulation, and predicted among other things the existence of pulmonary capillaries. It would be another 300 years before European scholars came to the same conclusion. As for the arts, there was Al-Mutannabbi's mesmerising poetry, Al-Kindi's influential philosophy and, much later, the inspirational fiction of Kalil Gibran. These and many other names are held up as shining stars in the history of Arabia, as well as they should be.

But I believe it is high time we shifted our gaze. While we venerate our forebears, it's imperative that we also identify and celebrate the present-day luminaries of the Arab world – those whose achievements beg for a fuller portrait of the figures behind them, whose tales of overcoming hardship, of forging ahead in the face of adversity, will undoubtedly serve to inspire young readers across the region. Now more than ever, the Arab world needs a new narrative, something to counter the prevailing perception of its people as primitive and prone to violence. It is my hope that by writing this book, I can help in some small way to bring that about.

Those doing the most, of course, are the subjects of this book, and to be honest, it was partly out of a desire to meet and learn about these impressive individuals, top performers across a spectrum of industries, that I set about the task of telling their stories. I've long admired them, and as I came to know them and their work, I felt compelled to share the details with a broader audience, to give these standouts the spotlight they all deserve. Right away, though, I realised I had a problem: there was far too little space to include them all. I would have to narrow my list of dozens down to just 10. I managed to do so, but what a challenge that was.

Over the following months, I sat down with each of them and recorded their stories — stories of success that almost always began with failure, stories of hard work and persistence, of missteps and misfortune, and, yes, often enough, of luck. I asked them how they had come to be where they are, what kind of setbacks they'd encountered along the way, and why they had gotten up when they fell down. I asked them what advice they would give to young people and what advice had helped them, and then I listened.

And what they said surprised me.

It wasn't the stories themselves, but rather how much they all had in common. Regardless of where they'd grown up — Jordan or Saudi Arabia, Tunisia or Lebanon or Bahrain — these men and women had confronted many of the same challenges, harboured many of the same fears, and struggled with the same doubts. Not one of them knew, upon starting out, where the journey would take them, or that it would all work out in the end. They all took risks, and at one point or another, one way or another, they all stumbled. But they all had a vision, and a burning passion for the work, and they were all determined to stay the course no matter what obstacles life threw in their way, and no matter how distant the finish line seemed.

I realised, too, how much their stories resembled my own. Having endured the deprivations of a pre-modern Oman, I know what it means to struggle. Especially being a former fighter pilot, I know well the pressures of performing, the terror and thrill of being alone at the controls, and the consequences of a miscalculation. At 450 knots, there was never time for fear; a fighter pilot is forced to be decisive, to act quickly, to hit the target on time, and in their own way, the Arab achievers I've profiled here have done just that – fearlessly, if figuratively, taking to the skies, executing plans, and learning to lead.

They are also a testament to the value of education. Without it, and without working hard to excel, none of these individuals would be where they are today. It's true that education in its current state isn't enough to guarantee employment, and that's a problem that people like Jordan's Soraya Salti, Executive Vice President of Injaz Al-Arab, and Tunisia's Lotfi Maktouf, founder and director of Almadanya, are working hard to address. But if Arab youth are to have any shot of realising their potential, education is imperative.

Joumana al Jabri and Ramzi Jaber

A Laboratory for Change

WE LIVE TODAY IN AN AGE OF INFORMATION ABUNDANCE. Humans, it has been estimated, will produce more data in the next five years than we have in the last 5,000 years. This might seem, on the face of it, a positive trend; more data can give us a clearer picture of the world around us, a better understanding of the issues we face, and smarter solutions to our most challenging problems. More information *can* be a very good thing.

But the data that surrounds us can also cloud our vision, obscuring the things we most urgently need to see, or overwhelm our senses, leading to fatigue and apathy. When it comes to matters of social justice, to the most pressing problems of our time, we can ill afford to let these stories slip away, unnoticed, and ultimately, forgotten. It's imperative that we develop a better means of delivering information and package the most important information in such a way that it's absorbed and remembered. This is precisely what Joumana al Jabri and Ramzi Jaber have set out to do.

As co-founders of the organisation, Visualizing Impact, al Jabri and Jaber, along with a highly committed team, are creating storytelling tools, designed to break through this information noise, and to transform reams of raw data on issues of social justice into impactful visuals, capable of rewiring the brain. It's innovative work, informed by evidence-based science, tells us that the human being is a visual creature; we respond emotionally to colour; we absorb information conveyed graphically more quickly than text, we retain it longer; and we connect more deeply, of course, with personal stories, than we do with abstract figures.

It was upon seeing one of these infographics, as they're called – a wonderfully illustrated comparison of Israeli and Palestinian ceasefire violation (the former far outweighing the latter), published in a leading news weekly – that I determined to find out who it was who had made it. I soon found myself face to face with this extraordinary duo.

Al Jabri, who currently splits her time between Dubai and Beirut, is identified as 'equally Syrian, Saudi, Lebanese, and Palestinian'. Central to her identity, she says, is the Arabic language. Jaber, on the other hand, was born in Jerusalem. Though he spent much of his youth abroad – Montreal, Paris, Dubai – his legal status in every country was always temporary. Due to restrictions on Palestinians who travel abroad, he now finds himself in the rather ridiculous position of being barred from visiting his own birthplace. But what they share in common – a background in the architecture and construction industry – is what brought them together.

The daughter of architects, al Jabri grew up immersed in the field. After earning her bachelor's degree in architecture and fine arts from the Rhode Island School of Design in the United States, she went on to Beirut, where she spent the next seven years practicing with Pierre Khoury Architects and Bernard Khoury. In time, al Jabri grew frustrated by the constraints of the Lebanese context, where she says architects are typically hired late in the process, requiring them to work within extremely limited parameters. There was also the fact that, in a place like Lebanon, long-term projects could easily be derailed by events beyond the architect's control – a conflict, say, or an attack, such as the one that killed former Prime Minister Rafik Hariri in 2005.

'That experience was a real turning point for me', says al Jabri, who was working with her partners on residential buildings in Beirut when the explosion ripped through Mr Hariri's motorcade in the city's downtown. 'After that', she says, 'the investors pulled out, and the project was scrapped'. A year later, it happened yet again. Al Jabri, along with her partners and a group of other creative companies in Lebanon, had rented a warehouse with the aim of converting it into a space to house those companies that would be open to the public. Construction was just about to begin when Israeli forces launched a ground invasion of southern Lebanon, setting off a 34-day war and scuttling their plans.

'After that, I knew I wanted to work through a process with incremental impact', she says. 'Where the work could affect change within a highly volatile context'. More than an aesthetic pursuit, design and creative processes, al Jabri knew, could serve as a powerful tool for solving problems; and problem solving, she realised, was her true passion.

Jaber, meanwhile, was pursuing his own plans. A structural engineer by training, he had recently left a job with a leading engineering firm in Dubai, where he had contributed to the design of the columns of the

'Dubai Pearl', a 73-story residential skyscraper still under construction. Had Jaber stayed on in that position, he most certainly would have enjoyed a successful career, well-salaried and comfortably situated in a city famous for its luxury accommodations.

Instead, Jaber sought out socially meaningful projects. Like al Jabri, he wanted to make a difference. How exactly he might do that, he wasn't sure. Then in 2009, on a trip to India, the answer came to him. After attending the TED India conference, Jaber was inspired to organise a TED event for Palestinians. It was in the course of doing so, he says, that he first met al Jabri, who had recently been laid off as a result of the financial crisis then unfolding in Dubai. What followed was the kind of professional collaboration that seemed to have been written in the stars – the coming together of likeminded thinkers with complementary skillsets and a common goal. 'We realised our visions are quite similar', says al Jabri, 'that we're driven by the same things.'

A PERFECT PAIRING

Over the next year, al Jabri and Jaber worked side-by-side to put their ideas into action. Given that roughly 7 out of 10 Palestinians are refugees or internally displaced people, they knew that the majority of those for whom the event was being organised would not be able to attend. 'So we were forced to be creative', Jaber told an audience at the TEDxSummit in Doha a year later. 'We decided to hold an event that spanned three countries to include Palestinians and others who otherwise wouldn't be able to speak or participate.' The conference, they decided, would be held simultaneously in Beirut, Bethlehem-Ramallah, and Amman, and live-streamed to 20 other cities around the world.

Designed to explore the Palestinian reality, to give it the texture and colour – even the factual information – often missing from accounts in the mainstream media, the event brought together an eclectic mix of writers, researchers, artists, and activists – people like the Palestinian lawyer and author Raja Shehadeh, who in 1979 founded the Arab world's first human rights organisation, Al-Haq (Law in the Service of Man), in the West Bank. Credited with bringing an international legal framework to bear on the Kafkaesque judicial system of the Occupied Territories, Al-Haq has, for decades, monitored and documented human rights violations by all parties to the conflict.

There was also the Pulitzer Prize-winning African-American novelist Alice Walker, the author of 'The Color Purple', and an outspoken critic of Israel's 'apartheid regime', who recalled her experiences in Australia and South Africa and 'the spirit of resistance and resilience' she found in those places – something she found in equal measure, she said, among the people of Palestine. The Brazilian documentarian Julia Bacha, who recounted the making of her award-winning film 'Budrus' about the poor West Bank village, where, at the height of the second intifada, non-violent demonstrators stood up to Israeli bulldozers, threatening the destruction of their community.

There was Khaled al Sabawi, founder and president of the green energy company MENA Geothermal, who described his company's efforts to install the largest geothermal system in the region at Jordan's University of Madaba as well as his personal quest to address Palestine's energy crisis – or as he puts it, 'to keep Palestine cool', and

Fadi Ghandour, the founder and former CEO of Aramex, the leading logistics andtransportation company in the Middle East, who talked about Ruwwad 'Entrepreneurs for Development', a private sector-led model for development that aims to empower communities through youth activism, civic engagement, and education.

And the list went on.

Still, for all of the star power, Jaber and al Jabri knew that if the event was to be embraced by the community, they would have to find a way to engage the Palestinian youth. Many young people, they knew, had become disillusioned with the education system, and few, it seemed, had ever heard of a TED Talk. So Jaber and the Ramallah team came up with a plan: they would drive a TEDx Ramallah school bus to universities throughout the West Bank. At each one, they would invite students to a screening of Sir Ken Robinson's 2006 TED Talk 'How Schools Kill Creativity', the most viewed TED Talk of all time and one particularly relevant to the long-suffering people of Palestine. Meanwhile, al Jabri and the Beirut team partnered with the youth newspaper Hibr Lubnani on a project, to include in the paper a monthly feature about an inspiring Palestinian refugee in Lebanon. Long after the event ended, Hibr Lubnani continued to run the feature.

TEDxRamallah turned out to be a major success, broadcasting far and wide stories of Palestinians' oppression and exile, courage and hope, and creating awareness worldwide. These stories had been silenced in favour of a media narrative, strongly sympathetic to the Israeli cause. The story of civil disobedience in Budrus, for example, had never made the news; only years later, when Bacha's film was released to critical acclaim, did the rest of the world learn of those extraordinary events, reflecting the confirmation bias that, Bacha argues, often colours coverage of the conflict – 'a tendency we all have as human beings to ignore things that challenge our notions about an issue.'

But these stories had also been hidden away, buried in voluminous, densely-worded documents, invisible to the average onlooker with little time on her hands to dig through the data. Even Jaber, himself a member of the Palestinian diaspora, had, at the time, only a vague idea of what was going on inside the occupied territories. One statistic he learned was that, on an average, every year since 2001, more than 500 Palestinian children have been detained by the Israeli military – stopped him in his tracks. 'I was shocked that I didn't know these numbers', he recalls. 'And yet, this is one of the well-documented causes on the planet.'

It was that ignorance of the facts on the ground, of the conflict in concrete figures, Jaber says, that moved him to pursue another pioneering project. 'Ramzi really seeded the idea of packaging data in the form of visual media, of using design to convey knowledge', al Jabri told me. 'So I joined him. I saw the tools' potential, and I realised that what we wanted to create was something unique – that there was nothing out there quite like it.' Storytelling is a venerated Arab tradition, Jaber told one interviewer. 'We wanted to augment it by harnessing the power of technology and design to reach a wider audience.'

VISUAL STORIES

In 2012, al Jabri and Jaber teamed up with several other creative professionals – among them, Ahmad Barclay,

Hani Asfour, Naji el Mir, Ahmad Ghunaim, and Morad Taleeb – to launch Visualizing Palestine (VP). Situated at the intersection of data science, technology, and design, the multidisciplinary team –researchers, communications experts, architects, designers, and techies – aimed to combine their collective skills in the production of infographics depicting a factual, rights-based narrative of the Israeli-Palestinian conflict through the lens of social justice. In more than three years since, they have done just that, adding a new dimension to the global discussion, empowering change agents around the world, and pushing the boundaries of conventional storytelling.

To date, VP's infographics have been published in such leading mainstream media outlets as The Washington Post, Al-Jazeera English, the Guardian, the Daily Beast, the Huffington Post, Fast Co., Jadaliyya, and others. They've appeared in books and magazines, on subway billboards and in international exhibitions, and they've been used by a wide variety of professionals, including university professors, students, journalists, social scientists, and activists in some 79 cities in 29 countries around the world. In 2014, Visualizing Palestine was presented with an 'award of distinction' at Ars Electronica, one of the largest and most distinguished art and technology festivals in the world, and a Best of Blogs 'Bobs') award for Best Social Activism by Deutsche Welle, Germany's international broadcaster. VP was also presented a Kantar Information is Beautiful community award in 2013 and an On Think Tanks Data Visualization Competition award in 2015. At the 2015 MIT Enterprise Forum Arab Startup Competition, VP won in the category for social entrepreneurship.

Before they could create a single image, though, the

VP team had to sift through a veritable mountain of data. In the five-year period between 2008 and 2012, Israel–Palestine was tied with China-and-Tibet as the second most reported on area by Human Rights Watch. Only the United States, where Human Rights Watch is based, was the subject of more reports. There were also the dozens of reports on the Israel and Palestine by other international agencies, including the United Nations, the World Bank, and Amnesty International, and by Israeli and Palestinian groups like B'tselem and Al-Haq, respectively.

Data collection was only part of the process. 'One of the main issues we address is the media narrative that is relaying those facts', al Jabri told an audience at Ars Electronica, citing an example of the bias prevalent in mainstream publications. 'This was the New York Times reporting 50 percent of Israeli children killed, and less than 10 percent of Palestinian children killed in 2004', she said, referring to an infographic entitled, 'You Can Handle the Truth', illustrating, in red and black, the two groups' starkly contrasting treatment. Moreover, she added, that narrative does much to shape public opinion, particularly in the United States. As another infographic made clear, in the midst of fighting in 2012, some 57 percent of the American public thought Israel's actions in Gaza were justified.

VP strives to counter those false narratives by humanising the numbers, says al Jabri. 'Data is dry and boring and often hard to remember, so we try to make them relevant to people like myself who are not Palestinian.' That means creating stories that connect with people on a personal level – that help them understand, for example, what it means to live in a segregated society, where one's freedom of movement is limited by a variety of barriers, both physical and legal. Such was the focus of one infographic titled 'Identity Crisis: The Israeli ID System', which went viral shortly after it was posted on social media, reaching more than 136,000 people in under a week.

Another, titled 'Uprooted', depicted the tremendous economic impact of Israel's destruction of Palestinian olive groves. 'Since 1967, Israeli authorities have uprooted 800,000 olive trees, equal to 33 Central Parks', read the caption, written over a 'Photoshopped' image of a bulldozer plowing through that leafy pleasure ground in the heart of Manhattan, which framed the problem in terms familiar to an American audience. The result: US$12.3 million in lost income each year to the 80,000 Palestinian families that rely on the olive harvest for their livelihood. To highlight the hypocrisy of 'peace talks', the VP team rendered a data-rich breakdown of what has been happening on the ground. Titled '20 Years of Talks: Keeping Palestinians Occupied', the infographic showed that since the Oslo Accords in 1993, the Israeli settler population had more than doubled, reaching roughly half a million, while the Israeli government had forced some 11,000 Palestinians out of Jerusalem and demolished more than 15,000 Palestinian homes.

Yet, perhaps, VP's most powerful piece was its very first: a deeply researched, visually arresting infographic chronicling the progression of a prolonged hunger strike. 'Day 15: mental sluggishness, standing up becomes difficult or impossible', read the caption. 'Day 28: 18% weight loss. Day 35: Fast, uncontrollable eye movements, incoercible vomiting. Day 45: Death can occur at any time due to heart failure.'

Al Jabri explained that the work was a response to the plight of Khader Adnan, the Palestinian who fasted for a staggering 66 days in protest of his detention without charge, or 'administrative detention' (Another VP infographic describes this practice in detail). It was only after 52 days that Adnan's strike was picked up by Al-Jazeera, its first mention in the mainstream media. Reuters ran an article on Day 59, followed by CNN and the New York Times three days later. When Adnan ended his hunger strike on Day 66, said al Jabri, the article that appeared in the New York Times led with a photo, not of Adnan, but of an anonymous masked man hurling a rock as plumes of black smoke rise from a nearby fire. Adnan was detained again in 2015.

That image had nothing to do with the story itself, al Jabri noted, but it reinforced an all too familiar stereotype of Palestinians. 'So what we did is take that and turn it into a story that is not only about Palestinians, but about the human being – about enduring a social injustice. We researched medical reports of what happens to the body, what is the maximum number of days one can strike, and who among those seen as peacemakers today has had to go through that.'

What began with Visualizing Palestine has since blossomed into the more broadly focussed Visualizing Impact. While al Jabri and Jaber continue their work on the former, they've also begun to expand the organisation's portfolio beyond the situation in Palestine and Israel to examine issues of social justice affecting other populations throughout the MENA region. 'We're refining our methodology', said al Jabri, 'and we hope that by sharing it with new partners, we can equip communities to generate collective action and build international solidarity around social movements.' Thus was born, last May, a new Egypt-focussed series of infographics on media censorship in the Arab world's largest country.

On May 3, World Press Freedom Day, Visualizing Impact, in partnership with the Cairo-based news website, Mada Masr, unveiled the first of the series' visuals. 'Shadowed Signals: The Practice of Censorship' attempts to document 'the structure of censorship' in Egypt, and how various practices – everything from the use of legal instruments to prosecute and intimidate journalists, to the manipulation of content by members of the media – prevent message dissemination. A marriage of Mada Masr's local knowledge and Visualizing Impact's expertise in concept-driven design, Visualizing Egypt demonstrates the vast potential for partnership going forward.

There might one day, for example, be a 'Visualizing Syria' or a 'Visualizing Women' or, as was recently proposed, a 'Visualizing Bangladesh' that would document the myriad social injustices perpetrated against the country's poor and marginalised. The possibilities are endless, but as al Jabri sees it, the success of any such collective endeavor will ultimately rest on the ability of individuals to question their own beliefs – 'on the change that can happen within an individual to allow them to reach their full potential and to have an impact on the issues that are important to them.'

Together with their team of creative professionals, Joumana al Jabri and Ramzi Jaber are using digital tools to powerful effect. By presenting raw data in the form of infographics, Visualizing Impact is able to challenge false narratives, illuminate important issues, and inform public debate, and in this, the organisation stands alone, a model of innovation with the potential to influence events far and wide.

Lotfi Maktouf
Almadanya

LONG BEFORE I MET LOTFI MAKTOUF, I WAS AN ADMIRER of Almadanya, the fantastic organisation he founded and runs in his native Tunisia.

Started in 2011, shortly after the uprising that sparked what would come to be known as the 'Arab Spring,' the non-political NGO empowers Tunisian citizens through a number of educational, developmental, and cultural programmes, aimed at addressing the root causes of that unrest: namely, chronic high unemployment, institutional corruption, and the decades-long disenfranchisement of the country's largely impoverished inland populations.

A highly successful lawyer turned international financier, Lotfi might seem an unlikely advocate for Tunisia's downtrodden and dispossessed. As evidenced by his hand-made suits, he owns and enjoys many of the markers of mega wealth. His collection of fine art and writing instruments, much of which he plans to donate to his native country, could fill a museum, and among his many assets are luxury hotels and famous agri-business brands. Still, for all of his worldliness and wealth, Lotfi knows well the deprivations endured by ordinary Tunisians. After all, he once was one.

Born in a village on the outskirts of the coastal town of Sousse, Lotfi struggled up from humble roots. For much of his youth, he shared a single small room with his parents and three siblings. His father, a civil servant, provided for the family what he could. But times were tough, and were it not for family and friends who knew the value of education, he says, 'I probably would never have made it out. The only reason I'm talking to you today is because a decision was made that I would go to school and study hard. I owe my success to that decision, to my education, and I don't owe it to anything else.'

Lotfi still recalls with bitterness his 'first real taste of institutional corruption'. Having graduated at the top of his class in college, he was due to receive a scholarship to continue his studies at the Sorbonne in Paris. But the scholarship that was rightly his was awarded instead to a classmate from one of Tunisia's 'politically connected' families. 'I felt powerless', he said. 'Like an outcast'. But undeterred, Lotfi continued on, paving his way at the Sorbonne by cleaning offices and working as a delivery boy. Life was early mornings and late nights, long days and little rest. There were times, to be sure, when doubt weighed him down, when he wondered if what his mother had always told him was true – if hard work really did pay off.

And then, one day, it did. It came as a letter in the mail, in a bulky envelope postmarked from Cambridge, Massachusetts in the United States. Mr Lotfi Maktouf, the letter said, had been accepted into the Harvard School of Law, would he kindly inform the admissions office of his intent to enroll. Lotfi dropped the letter in disbelief. Then he picked it up and read it again. 'We are pleased to inform you…' He did that again and then again. It wasn't until the third or fourth time, he says, that the shock subsided and the reality set in: he was going to Harvard – to *Harvard*. Just like that, he knew, a door, a very large door, had swung open, and a young Tunisian man, a humble, dark-skinned Arab student from a small country in North Africa, strode confidently through it, taking his place at one of the most esteemed educational institutions in the world.

After graduating from Harvard, Lotfi accepted an offer from one of the leading law firms on Wall Street. A 'rain-maker' as they call them on the Street, he had a bright future in the profession, and he might have well continued on that path, making partner, and enjoying a comfortable existence in Manhattan. But Lotfi had bigger plans. After several years in New York, he changed course, taking a senior position as Principal Counselor with the International Monetary Fund in Washington, D.C. There he specialised in advising countries emerging from political upheaval, helping them develop the monetary and fiscal reforms necessary to regain financial stability, and though he couldn't have known it at the time, Lotfi was preparing for a future role.

As Lotfi's fortunes grew, Tunisia's turned sour. For three decades, Habib Bourguiba, the republic's first president, had molded the nation into a modern state. With no lucrative natural resources to draw on – no oil or gas, no gold or diamonds – Tunisia, he knew, would have to invest in its people, and right away, the Western-educated leader set about that task. Under Bourguiba, liberal economic policies led to a flourishing of private enterprise, while an ambitious development programme fought poverty, built infrastructure, and broadened access to education – and not only for men. Indeed, among his sweeping reforms, Bourguiba's boldest measure was to include women as full participants in Tunisian society, giving them concrete rights still unheard of in the Arab world.

By the time Lotfi arrived at the IMF, an aging Bourguiba had left office. In his place was President Zine El Abidine Ben Ali, who, upon seizing control of the country, rolled back many of his predecessor's reforms. However, Bourguiba was educated, Ben Ali was not, and rather than invest in the Tunisian people, he made them prisoners of a police state, all the while enriching himself and his cronies at the public's expense. 'The Ben Ali regime was solely motivated by the prospect of financial gain', said Lotfi. 'Ben Ali had no long-term plans. He ruled the country as only an uneducated man can; by making sure that those under him remain ignorant. His iron grip suffocated the people.'

As Ben Ali's despotic governing style led the country down a dark path, Lotfi looked on with dismay. Like other expatriate Tunisians, he seethed with anger at what was happening, but he was powerless to do anything about it. Meanwhile in Tunisia, a feeling of discontent had begun to spread through the population. Over the next two decades, that feeling would slowly ferment, building up pressure until it found its release on 18 December, 2010. That day, a fruit seller in Tunis set himself on fire in a desperate act of protest, setting off the so called Jasmine Revolution.

What followed over the next eight weeks would transform the country. By January 14, Ben Ali had been forced from office, plunging Tunisia into uncharted waters.

Although Lotfi shared his countrymen's excitement at the strong man's ignominious exit, he knew that Tunisia faced a perilous period of instability over the months and years ahead. Politics abhors a vacuum, and lacking a developed civil society, Tunisia, he feared, would come under the control of extremist groups, like the long-banned Ennahda Islamic movement, who were poised and ready to fill it.

BIRTH OF A MOVEMENT

Lotfi watched from afar as the uprising unfolded, avidly following updates and constantly talking to friends in Tunisia. But in order to truly understand the situation and the country's most urgent needs, he knew he had to be there, on the ground, among the people. Thus, on January 17, just days after Ben Ali's departure, Lotfi landed in the capital, Tunis, accompanied by a small team and armed with a simple mission: 'I promised myself one thing', he said, raising an index finger for emphasis. 'I would not talk. I would only listen.'

Over the next seven weeks, Lotfi crisscrossed the country, chatting up shopkeepers, sitting in cafés, documenting the demands of the protesters – the slogans chanted on the streets and spray-painted on the walls. Sticking mainly to the poor, rural parts of the country, far from urban centres and the more cosmopolitan coast, he took the pulse of the Tunisian people in the midst of an extraordinary moment in their history. 'I felt it was important to record what they were literally crying out for during this time of upheaval', he said, 'because that's what they really wanted and it would soon be forgotten.'

What Lotfi found, he says, was both heartening and worrying. On the one hand, underpinning the uprising were three democratic demands – freedom, dignity, and employment – that could move the country, he believed, in a positive direction. But there were signs too, he noted, that certain elements sought to exploit the anger and frustration at Ben Ali's corrupt regime for their own self-serving ends. 'Everywhere I visited, Ennahda, the Islamist movement, had already been there before me', he recalled. 'And by the time I'd finished my trip, there was a very perturbing shift from these three pillars of the revolution to more faith-related demands.'

Based on his research, Lotfi concluded that what Tunisians needed most were the civil institutions necessary for consolidating democratic gains. And the only way to achieve that, he knew, was through education. 'To extremists, an educated women is a threat', said Lotfi. 'One of the most important responsibilities of a mother is to pass her knowledge on to her children – to educate the next generation. But if she is uneducated, her children will grow up to be ignorant, and ignorance, we all know, is a fertile ground for religious indoctrination.' Only by educating women and providing them with the same opportunities granted to men could Tunisians hope to tame extremism and nurture economic growth.

Once back in Monaco, Lotfi invited a group of close business, academic, and financial managers to discuss his findings and to challenge the civil empowerment strategy he had designed for going forward – a means of assisting the Tunisian people to realise their potential and fulfill their aspirations. That meeting went on for hours, he said, and the ideas came pouring out. 'We had a number of very impressive proposals, and from that, we came up with the final layout and the programmes that comprise the work of my foundation.' Thus was born Almadanya. Named after the Arabic word for 'civil', and Almadanya went to work right away, opening four offices and launching key programmes targeting the neediest populations.

As Lotfi explained when we met, the Almadanya pursues its mission through a wide variety of activities – everything, from smoothing the way for foreign investment in Tunisia and strengthening independent media, to preserving the country's cultural heritage, protecting the environment, providing vocational training to the unemployed, and assisting small farmers in securing access to regional and international markets. Yet, guiding all of its work, says Lotfi, are two fundamental principles: that men and women are equal and deserve the same opportunities, and that access to quality education is imperative, both for individual advancement and social progress. 'There is no future without these', he says.

One of the first programmes to get up and running was 'License to Dream', which helps young unemployed students obtain driver's licenses. Traditionally, a very costly and time-consuming ordeal in Tunisia, obtaining a license is a necessary first step for driving a truck, tractor or other kinds of machinery. As a result, poor people, particularly those in rural areas, were often deprived of this means of generating income. In the first province Almadanya approached, representatives of the area's driving schools told Lotfi they had issued around 70 licenses over the previous 6 weeks. Almadanya bought spaces for 200 more students on the spot, but only on the condition that all students were unemployed and that half of them were women. Since then, the number of licensees exceeds two thousand, and all of those individuals subsequently found jobs. 'For many of these youth, it's the first ID card they've ever had of their own volition', says Lotfi. 'So it's also a real source of pride.'

Another programme called 'Fatma; fights school dropout by providing free transportation for children living between 5 and 13 kilometres from the nearest school. While in urban areas of Tunisia, roughly 50 percent of young people stop going to school before completing their secondary education. The problem is even worse in rural parts of the country, where more than 80 percent of boys and 85 percent of girls drop out of school early, according to a recent report by the World Bank. Named for its first beneficiary, 'Fatma' has so far served more than 6,000 boys and girls, says Lotfi, giving them daily access to an education that could change their lives, just as it did his.

There's also 'Dar Almadanya' which offers free short-term accommodation to parents attending to their ill or injured children at the Central Pediatric Hospital in Tunis, and a programme called 'Baladi' (Arabic for 'my town') which provides each municipality in Tunisia with its own website. 'In today's world, accurate, up-to-date, easily accessible information is critical', says Lotfi, explaining that the content of each site is developed by residents and local authorities. Baladi offers visitors and potential investors a clear and honest picture of the municipality's hotel offerings, its schools and hospitals, bazaars and amusement centres, information on any ongoing infrastructural projects, and a calendar of events.

In an effort to promote learning and preserve Tunisia's national heritage, Almadanya has undertaken an ambitious programme to design, build, and manage 10 museums, even offering to take over the management of state-run museums that have fallen into disrepair (An art enthusiast,

Lotfi has plans to donate a number of pieces from his personal collection to a future museum). In the same vein is 'Roots', a programme designed to educate young people about their origins and heritage. In collaboration with Tunisian's Education Authority, Almadanya designs, organises, and funds educational excursions to sites of historical significance across the country – places like El Jem, with its stunning Roman ruins, and the ancient city of Carthage, Rome's chief rival, which was founded by the Phoenecians in the 9th Century BC.

Courtesy of Almadanya, thousands of children have also visited the Bardo National Musuem in Tunis. One of the most important museums in the Mediterranean, the Bardo was the target of a terrorist attack in March 2015. But that did nothing to deter Lotfi from his mission. On the contrary, in the wake of that attack, he instructed programme managers to take even more pupils to visit the Bardo.

'We all know travel broadens the mind', says Lotfi. 'Some of these children leave their town or village for the first time on these trips, so the journey itself is often just as important as the places they visit.'

One of the most pressing problems in Tunisia – and around the world – is also one of the least understood. Desertification, or the degradation of dryland ecosystems by intensive farming and overgrazing, affects close to 80 percent of the country's land, with serious implications for socio-economic stability. When the land can no longer support agriculture and groundwater has been exhausted, the local population migrates to urban areas in search of increasingly scarce jobs. Almadanya is partnering with the Ministry of Agriculture to address the menace of desertification by planting 1 million trees in the most severely affected areas. Till date, more than 1,50,000 trees have been planted and Almadanya is in the process of expanding Green Tunisia to rural schools by encouraging students themselves to plant trees in their school courtyards.

SAVING TUNISIA

'Tunisia has existed for millennia', Lotfi told me, his eyes flashing with intensity as he thumbed through his book, occasionally plucking out passages to reinforce a point. Published in French in 2011, *Saving Tunisia* (Fayard 2011) is both a paean to the country's proud history, its cultural riches and contributions to the world, and a prescription for navigating the turbulent waters of its current transition.

'It was Carthage — first Punic, then Roman, and eventually Christian — that established Tunisia at the nexus of perpetual negotiation between East, West, and Africa', he said. 'By 698, the Arabs had invaded and taken control, finding a land rich in history, and they built the illustrious Zaytuna mosque.' Said to be the oldest teaching establishment in the Arab world, the Zaytuna was responsible for training Tunisia's elite, and served as a bellwether for progress.

A melting pot of religions and ethnicities, Tunisian society flourished for centuries, with the Zaytuna emerging as one of the Islamic world's most important centres of learning. Scholars of theology, jurisprudence, history, science, and medicine, flocked to the school from around the known world, drawn as they were to its large libraries housing tens of thousands of books, including a large collection of rare manuscripts. Among the Zaytuna's graduates were such notable figures as Ibn Khaldun, regarded as a founding father of modern sociology, historiography, and economics; the encyclopedist Ahmad Ibn Youssef Ibn Ahmad Ibn Abubaker Tifashi; the Tunisian national poet Aboul-Qacem Echebbi; and the renowned Arabist and judge M.T Ben Achour.

Yet, by the 19th Century, he writes, Arab-Muslim Tunisia had begun its descent into a prolonged period of 'impoverishment, epidemics, ignorance, and economic exhaustion'. Whereas, the Zaytuna had once embraced fresh ideas, it became 'a bastion of conservatism', and rather than encourage its students to study the sciences or foreign languages, the university confined itself to reading and explicating the Koran, producing graduates unfit for leadership.

Not until Bourguiba took office, did the country begin to recover. 'By making people its first priority, Tunisia created a unique model of development and growth', Lotfi writes, describing how in less than three decades, the leader's investments had paid off: 'Tunisia had become a peace-loving, rapidly-developing country, with a healthy, educated population, relatively decent infrastructure, prudent management of public finances, an expanding middle class, and a coherent, realistic, diplomatic policy.'

Yet, above all, he says, it was the emancipation of women, and the compulsory schooling of girls, that paved the way for Tunisia's emergence as a modern Arab state, unique in the MENA region. Laws guaranteeing equality of the sexes not only endowed women with new rights, including the right to initiate divorce, the right to family planning services and contraceptives, the right to have an abortion, and freedom of movement, but they also set the tone for a host of other social programmes, facilitating co-education, for example, and mingling of the sexes in public places.

As a result, Tunisian women were at the forefront of the country's resistance movement, and they remain today the loudest voices in opposition to the governing Ennahda party, says Lotfi, 'for the simple reason that they are the ones who stand to lose the most.'

Looking back, Lotfi ruefully notes that the predictions he made in the book have unfortunately come to pass. Since the uprising in 2011, four interim governments have come and gone, unemployment is up, and prices continue to rise as the economy falters. Tunisia, he says, is trapped in an identity crisis, a challenge 'of historic and existential dimensions.' The imposition of what he calls an 'Islamist protocol' represents 'an unacceptable form of authoritarianism that is bound to fail.'

No matter how daunting the forces are of extremism, says Lotfi, the Tunisian people know who they are. As he learned from listening to them, they're ready to carry on with the unfinished work that Bourguiba began. 'I think Bourguiba did a fantastic thing', he says. 'I'm a product of it and I want to duplicate it, because I know for a fact that when you provide people with an education, its books, not bombs.'

An unseen star of the Arab world, Lotfi is a living proof of the transformative power of education. The son of a poor civil servant, he doggedly pulled himself up to heights even he could never have imagined as a young boy in Tunisia; and rather than resting on his laurels, he pressed ahead, determined to make a difference in the world. Almadanya is that. 'Our mission is to inspire Tunisians to dare, to begin the work today that will allow our youth to live a better tomorrow.'

Mohammed Saeed Harib

Freej

BEFORE HE WAS FAMOUS, BEFORE HE HAD SIGNED HIS first autograph or been surrounded by fans – before the idea for FREEJ had ever crossed his mind – Mohammed Saeed Harib was a below-average student in Boston, Massachusetts.

A freshman at Northeastern University, Mohammed had left the comforts of his home in Dubai only to find himself adrift in America, rudderless and far from family. His parents had hoped he would follow the well-beaten path so many bright Emiratis had taken before him: to a safe degree – in business, say, or engineering – and then, a stable, high-salaried job in the UAE's booming private sector.

For a time, Mohammed tried to meet those expectations. He chose architecture as his major, and he worked as hard as he played. But things didn't go as planned; Mohammed failed his first year class, and was kicked out of the programme. Recalling the moment decades later, he remembers dreading the conversation he would have to have with his father. Admitting that he'd failed out of architecture was one thing. But even harder, he says, was declaring that he would switch his major to the general arts.

'There was so much pressure from my family, and then there was the pressure I put on myself', he says. 'I kept asking myself, is this the right decision? Should I really do this? In a group of a hundred Emiratis there, I was the *only* art student.'

Mohammed followed his heart. At his core, he had always been creative. As a boy, he would sit with his cousins at their house in Dubai, and for hours on end, they would invent new games, weave wild narratives, and set off on adventures to fictional, faraway worlds. 'I loved to imagine stories and characters', he recalls. Yet, one thing Mohammed could never imagine, he says, was that he might one day parlay that creativity into a real-world career.

As an arts major, Mohammed was required to take a course in animation. 'One of the assignments was to come up with a superhero that represents your culture', he says. 'And my first attempt was the kind of a macho crime fighter you find in comic books.' Unimpressed, Mohammed's professor pushed him to dig deeper, to reflect on his roots. 'So, I started thinking about the person who had most inspired me – my grandmother – and her journey from the harsh conditions of her youth to present-day Dubai. Which is, of course, a very different place.'

Thus was born 'Um Saeed', the foundational character for what would one day become the Middle East's first 3D animated TV series – the path-breaking and wildly popular show known as FREEJ. In creating Um Saeed, the eldest and wisest of the four 'fun old girls' around whom the show revolves, Mohammed was merely paying homage to his grandmother; 'Um' is Arabic for 'the mother of', and 'Saeed' is his father's name.

But he soon realised that his superhero could be something more – that through her, he could speak to audiences of every age, and that he could celebrate, at once, the dynamism of the UAE and the ages-old traditions at risk of disappearing in the face of rapid modernisation.

First aired during Ramadan in 2006, FREEJ was an instant hit. Audiences across the Arab world tuned in to watch the band of gossiping grandmothers, all bedecked in Bedouin face masks. There's the sweet, slow-thinking Um Saloom; the tall, techy Um Allawi; and the always angry Um Khammas, the crude one constantly banging on about this or that, and of course, Um Saeed, the classic Bedouin figure, a wise old woman well-versed in traditional sayings and fluent in sarcasm. Together, over coffee in a quiet enclave of the city, they grapple with problems big and small, old and new, and never in harmony.

'[FREEJ] has gained the region-wide, cross-generational popularity of an Arab "Simpsons"', declared the Economist, noting that the show's 'depiction of raucous and irreverent Arab matriarchs has proved to be a revelation.' Indeed, within weeks, it was clear that Mohammed was onto something big – that beyond being a novel form of entertainment, FREEJ could inspire in viewers a deep emotional response, a feeling of attachment to characters who, even as cartoon caricatures, embody as well as any the Emirati identity.

In recognition of that achievement, Mohammed was awarded the Emerging UAE Talent Award at the 2007 Dubai International Film Festival. Later that year, he accepted a Special Country Award for the first season of FREEJ at the Hamburg Animation Awards, and in 2008, he was named Young CEO of the Year by CEO Middle East magazine. In the seven years since, Mohammed has followed up that early success with four more seasons of the show, establishing FREEJ as a household name across the Middle East.

Indeed, though he had never studied business, Mohammed has managed to build a very big one. As the chairman of Lammtara Art Production, the company he founded in 2005, one year before FREEJ first hit the air, he oversees a cast of more than 500 employees. Yet, even as he captains that ship, an operation of many moving parts, Mohammed remains the creative force driving it forward. 'From the start, I knew I did not want to specialise in just one thing', he says. 'I wanted to be a jack of all trades, and, in time, an ace in a few of them.'

That he is. Hands-on at each stage of the production process, Mohammed has honed his skills in everything, from photography to acting. 'I've picked up bits of knowledge from here and there', he says. 'And when you combine that with creative energy, the sky is the limit.' On top of all that, Mohammed also works with the screenwriters to finalise the script for every episode. 'It's a feeling', he says. 'It could come from a line of poetry, or a phrase, or just an idea – and we build the show around it.' FREEJ fans, it seems, can't get enough.

THE COMEBACK KID

The Lammtara studio, a renovated warehouse in central Dubai, resembles the sleek art galleries that line the same street: high ceilings, stone floors, modernist décor. In the main foyer, above a long glass table Mohammed designed himself, is a framed print of Um Allawi in the style of the Mona Lisa. When I visited the studio last fall, the team was hard at work on Season 5, fine-tuning every last detail – the colour of trees, the sound of a fountain – while Mohammed floated from room to room, crouching over shoulders, fielding questions, conducting the orchestra.

'I love going to my office', he told me. 'Because it's *my* office, I give more. I am a much more productive person'. But in the UAE, he said, few nationals choose that path. 'The state has provided them with a safety net; it's very easy to get a government job, which pays very well.' Working in the private sector can be, by comparison, quite hard. 'And creating your own company', he added, grinning. 'Well, that's even harder.'

For Mohammed, success didn't come easily. Conceiving FREEJ was one thing. Convincing Dubai's media executives to embrace his vision of a 3D animated show starring septuagenarians sipping coffee, slinging insults and solving society's problems, was quite another. None had ever aired an animated show. It didn't help matters that Mohammed was an industry novice no more familiar with a financial model than he was with the Periodic Table. 'I was an artist, so the numbers were very foreign to me', he says. 'But I was blessed to be working in Dubai Media City, which had a lot of experience developing business plans for media projects.'

Mohammed first shared the idea with the CEO of Dubai Media City, who took it on as a kind of experiment in new media. After a brief assessment, the budget came back at $2 million. 'That's enough to scare anyone', he says, particularly in an industry with no experience in animation and a dearth of original programming. 'They were simply importing shows from America and dubbing them, and we knew that people weren't satisfied with this – that many Emirates wanted to see quality, locally produced content about their own culture.'

Though the CEO of Dubai Media City loved the idea, he couldn't come up with $2 million, and urged Mohammed to explore ways he could bring that number down, perhaps by working with other companies. 'So I did', he says. 'I read everything I could find, I talked to experts, and I travelled around the region to figure out how we could make FREEJ for as cheaply as possible.' After three full years of exhaustive research, Mohammed had managed to trim the budget by about half, and, at last, he says, persistence paid off. 'I had been knocking on their door for three years. Finally they said, OK, enough. Our job is to support you if your business makes sense, and, well, it's a wild one, alright – but we think it does.'

Still, he says, it was only a loan. 'They gave me all the money, and in 5 years, I had to give it all back, plus 5 per cent interest.' Right away, Mohammed set about work, rushing to make his long-held vision a reality; and then, as luck would have it, another media group emerged on the scene. 'It happened to be right before my show was to go on air', he says. 'So I found myself nicely positioned between two telecom companies in a bidding war for this new idea, for the Arab world's first ever cartoon.' Up till then, Mohammed had only ever hoped he could cover his costs. By the time the first episode was broadcast, he had not only paid back the loan but had made 1 million dirham.

If there were any lingering doubts about how well the show would do, or that Arab audiences might not take so easily to a cartoon, the first season of FREEJ put those doubts to rest. In 2006, the year the UAE was first introduced to Um Saeed and her merry band of masked grannies, FREEJ was far and away the most watched show in the land. In fact, so strong were the season one ratings, that the station, Sama Dubai, promptly commissioned two more.

To all but Mohammed, FREEJ was an improbable success; its first run a wildly impressive feat few believed he could really pull off, and as such, its creators had lived up to their name. As he explained to me when I visited the studio, Mohammed is an avid enthusiast of horse racing, and Lammtara, which translates, roughly, to 'You ain't seen nothin' yet,' was the name of the champion colt owned by. 'I was very excited when Sheikh Mohammed decided to bring a group of horses from Europe to see whether or not they could train here in Dubai for the English Derby,' he says. 'The stables were just across the road from our own.'

One of those horses was a juvenile that had run only once before and had won his race. 'He was so young and inexperienced, you couldn't really know how good this colt would turn out to be.; A few months before the big race, Mohammed, then 16, paid a visit to the stable on an 'open day' when the public are permitted entry. Strolling along the track, he glimpsed from a distance that unmistakable chestnut coat, and asked the trainer leading him along if that was Lamtara. "'Yes, it is', he said, 'but he is very sick, I don't know if he'll make it.' Suffering from a lung abscess, Lammtara had been on the verge of death. To Mohammed's eyes, he was tiny, 'very much like me', he says. 'I thought that might be the last anyone would ever see of him.'

Several months later, the English Derby finally rolled around, and there, at the starting gate, was Lammtara, making his seasonal debut. 'I couldn't believe it', Mohammed recalled. 'He had not run a single race that year.' Slow out of the gate, Lammtara lost a shoe and lagged behind the pack. 'He was in the last place, and then he flew home', said Mohammed. 'He broke a 60-year-old record that day, and he never lost a race. I thought, wow, what an amazing horse – he came to Dubai, he recovered from an injury and a serious illness, and then he proved everyone wrong.

'Lammtara was so determined', said Mohammed. 'Nothing could keep him down, and I thought, you know, my story really isn't so different.'

STAYING ON TOP

After three successful seasons, Mohammed needed a break. He had been so fast out of the gate, had such an impact from the very start, that the expectations he'd created the demand for more and more and more, had begun to test his limits. Having laboured so long and hard to get the show off the ground, to launch a pioneering enterprise unlike anything the Arab world had ever seen, he was suddenly confronted with a challenge he hadn't anticipated.

'You have to continuously innovate', he says. Although in its second and third seasons, FREEJ was still the number one show in Arabia, 'nothing could ever match the magic of that first one', he says. 'It just can't be as good.' Worried that he would spend the rest of his career chasing a ghost, and going only downhill, Mohammed took a radical step. Risking the wrath of FREEJ fans everywhere, and putting in some peril the brand he had built from scratch, the artist-turned-executive decided to take a year off. He would rest and recharge, and then he would return.

No one, not even Mohammed, could have predicted the turn things would take over the next few months. With time to himself, he was able to tap more deeply into the well of creativity that had spawned FREEJ in the first place. If there was one way to top that feat, he knew, it was with an equally ambitious undertaking, something as big and bold as his much-loved masterpiece. 'So I jumped mediums', he says. 'We tried to do for theatre what we did for TV.' The result was, in its own way, no less impressive.

Indeed, just when everyone thought his best work was behind him, Mohammed followed up the region's first-ever cartoon TV show with the largest-ever Arabic theatrical production – a dazzling, over-the-top event, held to celebrate the UAE's 41st National Day in December, 2012. Performed at Dubai's Ductac Mall of the Emirates, 'Freej Folklore' combined dance, drama, film and animation with a live score by the London Philharmonic for 'a magical journey of discovery through the myths and legends of Arabia.'

If Arab audiences are unaccustomed to theatre, they didn't show it; some 20,000 spectators turned out to see 'Freej Folklore' over the course of the show's 10-day run, and critics were full of praise: 'Cirque du Soleil meets DreamWorks', declared *The National*, and 'Impressive doesn't even start to do it justice', gushed *Gulf News*. For Mohammed, though, the greatest endorsement of all was the deal that came about as a direct result of that directorial debut: an agreement with the Government of Dubai to create a Freej Theme Park, in exchange for a 30 per cent stake in his company.

'That was basically Nirvana', he says. 'Five years before, I was struggling to get a loan, and now I had my own theme park.'

Unfortunately, the financial crisis forced the government to scale back or cancel a number of projects, and plans for the park were eventually scrapped. But Mohammed knew Freej had a bright future nonetheless, and decided to take another year off to pursue different projects. One of them was directing the UAE's National Day Celebration. Mohammed's selection marked the first time in the country's history that a UAE national had been tapped to take the reins of the big event. 'It had always been a foreign company', he says. 'That was really the highlight of my career as an event director.'

He also used the time off to make his first foray into film – and at the international level no less. Mohammed was one of the 9 directors from around the world selected to contribute to a movie adaption of Khalil Gibran's *The Prophet* by executive producer Salma Hayek. Written and directed by Roger Allers, the director of 'The Lion King', the film features individual 'chapters' directed by acclaimed animators, all of them Oscar nominees and winners of distinguished awards. 'I'm the only guy who didn't win anything', Mohammed laughs. 'It was such a treat to work with a group of legends like that, and to meet Salma Hayek, who told me she really liked my chapter.'

Months later, Mohammed came back with the fourth season of FREEJ. 'Whenever you're out of the game that long, people tend to forget about you', he says. 'But people never forgot about us, and that's the mark, I think, of a very strong brand.' It's also a testament to Mohammed himself, to his remarkable talent, and to the persistence he practices and preaches. Indeed, once a month, Mohammed speaks at universities around the GCC. He doesn't take fees, and he doesn't do it because it looks good. He does it, he says, because he's convinced of one thing: that students need to be inspired – their eyes opened to the myriad opportunities at their fingertips.

'We're in a place in the world that is booming', he says. 'This is a chance to reach for your dreams. Don't give up before you've even tried. How many times did they tell me No? You have to believe in yourself. You have to have the courage to defend your ideas. And you have to be persistent. That's the message I always try to send', he says. 'I just hope they're listening. Because we need them – we need those young people who can dream, and who won't give up when someone older or more experienced tells them 'No.'

When life closed one door, Mohammed Harib found the courage to open another, to chart his own course. In creating FREEJ, he forged the blueprint for a novel genre of TV, while at the same time, paying homage to his forebears, the heroines of his native U.A.E. More than an illustrator, more than an entrepreneur, Mohammed is a visionary, someone who looks at the world and sees not only what is there, but also what isn't, and crucially, what can be.

Mutassem al-Sharji
The Enriching Experience

A LOVE OF LEARNING

SOCIAL MEDIA, IT'S CLEAR, IS NOW THE WAY OF THE WORLD. Facebook and Twitter, Instagram and LinkedIn, WhatsApp and Vine, and the list goes on: in countries across the globe, these online sites are gathering momentum where connections are made and communities come together; where ideas are exchanged and knowledge is acquired; where companies find their customers, and advertisers reach their audience; and Oman is no exception.

Indeed, every year, more and more Omanis – companies and individuals alike – are using these digital tools to enhance the way they do business or to network with potential employers. Some use social media to showcase their work or to broadcast their views on a particular topic – others simply to catalogue photos and keep in touch with family and friends.

To be sure, social media can be a boon to one's career and a fast and efficient way to keep up with the news. But at what cost do we live our lives online? What is it that we forfeit for the speed and convenience of the Internet? Is there something special, something essential even, about the face-to-face encounter? Could it be that this – the company of our peers, interaction in the flesh, talking and listening to other human beings – is as important to learning, to the growth of the mind, as the information itself?

Mutassem al-Sharji, for one, believes that it is, and it was that conviction that first led him to venture off the beaten path – to leave a safe career in economics for the opportunity to embark, as he puts it, 'on a journey of self-discovery'. Where exactly that journey would take him, Mutassem could hardly have known. But of one thing he was certain: he had to go. Life had become far too comfortable, too predictable, and too easy, and if his destination was uncertain, Mutassem knew well how to get there.

'Ever since I was a kid, my passion has been intellectual growth', Mutassem told me during one of our conversations, explaining that it was his father, a petroleum engineer and a man of wide-ranging interests, who first opened his eyes to the joys of learning. 'He was my first teacher', he recalled. 'We grew up in Muscat, and he had built in our house this enormous library. He always encouraged us, me, and my siblings, to use it – to read as much as possible'. Although an engineer by profession, his father was well-versed in a variety of other fields, he says – geology, linguistics, religion, biology and more. 'He actually memorised the entire Qur'an. It took him 15 years.'

That love of learning rubbed off on Mutassem, who shared his father's innate curiosity about the world. I took his advice to heart', he says. A voracious reader, Mutassem too devoured every book he could get his hands on –

everything from Eastern philosophy to Greek mythology to poetry and works of literature. As a student, he was always at the top of his class, with perfect marks on every report card through the 5th grade.

'But it's interesting', he says. 'I was also a bit of a rebel. At one point, I started thinking, you know, what am I trying to prove? And that's when I stopped studying.' Of course, Mutassem's curiosity never abated, and though he seldom prepared his school examinations, he didn't need to: so well-read was Mutassem in general that he managed to remain in the top three of his class through graduation. More than personal achievement, though, it was personal growth that Mutassem most valued – and that fuelled the development, years later, of his pioneering social enterprise: the Enriching Experience.

It all started, he says, in February 2013. Mutassem had long felt there was something missing in his day-to-day routine. For all of the wondrousness of the Internet, for all of the dialogue and debate fostered by social media sites like Facebook and Twitter, it seemed to Mutassem that the real world – life *offline* – was mostly void of intellectual discussion. Few were the forums in which one could truly learn from other individuals. Sure, there was the occasional social gathering, where friends and family might talk about the latest news, or share their thoughts about a movie, an informal chat between bites. But these invariably devolved into unproductive debates, as emotions prevailed over ideas, and winning – not *learning* – was often the real objective.

Having endured plenty of these sessions in his own life, Mutassem realised he probably wasn't alone. How many others, he wondered, were frustrated with the status quo?

How many others craved an opportunity to discuss subjects with people as intellectually curious as they? It occurred to Mutassem that if he could just cultivate the right environment, the right setting for scholarly engagement, he could offer something not even the most sophisticated software ever could – a chance to take a step back, to ignore, for a moment, the myriad digital distractions of our ever- connected lives, and silence the noise. 'In essence, to have discussions in a manner, and with certain values, that would ensure the best experience in terms of sharing and receiving knowledge for all', says Mutassem.

Of course, as with any out–of–the–box idea, it was hard to know if what he had envisioned on paper would actually work. So Mutassem decided to run it by a test audience of his cousins. 'Not knowing what to expect or how the meeting would turn out to be, we all decided to give a shot', he recalls. 'Three topics were put forward for a vote on which should be the focus of the first meeting's discussion.' Together, they decided on a time and place: 4:30 pm at Barbera Café in Bait Al Reem, Muscat; and thus was born, The Enriching Experience.

'By the end of the meeting, each and every one of the participants had recognised they had this enormous potential to learn and share knowledge – potential that wasn't apparent before the meeting', recalls Mutassem. 'No one had seen the greatness that lies within themselves.' Buoyed by the successful results of that first meeting, Mutassem and his cousins continued to meet every two weeks. At each meeting, they rotated the role of Chairperson, who suggests topics for voting and moderates the discussion in keeping with a set of seven values, the first letters of which spell out the word LITERAL.

Love to seek knowledge; Inclusiveness of everyone; Tolerance of all ideas; Respect for one another; Appreciation for everyone attending the meeting; and *Love to share knowledge.*

To help participants uphold those values, the Chairperson passes around the 'ball of wisdom', says Mutassem, explaining that only the person holding the ball has the floor to speak. In this way, he says, the meetings endow participants not only with new knowledge, but also with the confidence to express themselves before an audience of their peers – something that many of them had never before done.

'I knew some of our members through social media, where they had been very active', he says. 'They could express themselves very clearly and articulately in writing.' But upon seeing them at meetings, Mutassem noticed that those same individuals were far less outspoken in person. 'In fact, they were quite shy', he says. 'It was difficult for them at first.' But with a few months of practice, he says, they were able to overcome their inhibitions. 'They discovered in themselves a talent for speaking they didn't know they had. Now they're able to express themselves as confidently in person as on paper.'

NEW HORIZONS

When he was 18 years old, Mutassem set off on a trip that would change his life. Never before had he left Oman. Indeed, for all he had read about different countries, for all of the places his imagination could conjure, he had only ever truly known his own home. His family, his friends, his classmates: all shared the same language, the same religion, the same set of experiences. Only in books could he find people who were different. Yet reading, Mutassem knew, would only take him so far. To really grow as a person, he would have to leave the comforts of home for another culture, and upon graduating from high school, Mutassem decided to do just that, choosing to attend a university in Australia.

It was a big step. For a while he could count on his father to pay for the first two years of university, but he knew he would have to find a way to pay for the rest of his tuition by himself. He recalled a conversation with his father, 'a person who deeply values education', during his season year of high school, after Mutassem learned that he hadn't received a scholarship to study abroad. 'He told me: Son, I didn't anticipate that I'd have to pay for your education – I could send you at my own expense for the first year and, with some difficulty, for the second. But then you're on your own. So, if you decide to go ahead with this, you may not be able to continue your studies in Australia. Do you want to take that risk?'

Mutassem was worried. But he knew in his gut that it was the right move. 'Yes, I'm willing to take that risk', he told his father. 'I want to go'. A few weeks later, he was on his way to Perth for his freshman year at Curtin University of Technology.

'That was a completely new experience for me'. Mutassem recalls his time at Curtin. 'When I arrived, I made it my mission to seek out people of different backgrounds with different ways of thinking, different cultures and religions, and not only in the classroom, but through sports and social activities as well.' One of the most memorable friends Mutassem made, he says, was a young Chilean student named Francisco. 'He influenced me hugely', remembers Mutassem. 'He was very open-minded, very tolerant of others' views – and he pushed me to think differently myself.'

Mutassem excelled at Curtin. Having found support for his studies from Oman's Ministry of Higher Education, which covered his tuition for the entire four-year programme, Mutassem took full advantage of the opportunity. A major in finance and strategic economic analysis, he studied hard, of course, and did well in his classes. But just as importantly, he managed to make new friends, and to carve out time for extracurricular, including volunteer work with organisations serving the local community. In fact, Mutassem was selected from amongst more than 300 applicants to participate in the John Curtin Leadership Academy, the university's prestigious outreach programme aimed at developing the 'game changers of tomorrow.'

Only those students in the top 1 per cent of their graduating class are eligible for the JCLA. 'And I was actually the first Arab student to participate and graduate from the programme', says Mutassem, explaining that participants are required to find and support projects that benefit society at large. 'We supported some great organisations', he says, including one called Paws for Diabetics, a non-profit group that trains dogs to alert their owners before their blood sugar levels dip dangerously low. 'Life was hectic then', he recalls. 'I was so busy studying, working, and volunteering around the clock – but I loved it.'

Mutassem also made time to hone his karate skills. A longtime practitioner of martial arts, he had first learned karate at the age of 12, when his friend Khalil insisted he come along to a class. At the time, Mutassem was sceptical. 'Karate?' he'd said, rolling his eyes. 'That's just for spoiled kids who can't defend themselves. No thanks.' Looking back on it now, though, he acknowledges that he had been close-minded. Fortunately, Khalil persisted: 'Come on, let's give it a try', he said. 'We've got nothing to lose.' Mutassem, moved by the same curiosity that had made him such an avid reader, finally agreed to join him.

'And boy', he says, 'what a journey that has been'. Over the next 10 years, Mutassem would go on to embrace karate, practising it with a devotion bordering on obsession. Drawn to the sport's structure and discipline, he found in it not only a means for staying fit but, more importantly, a set of principles by which to live his life and a source of courage to take on any challenge. If it was curiosity that led Mutassem to learn about karate in the first place, it was toughness and perseverance, both mental and physical, which allowed him to stay the course – to push on through the greuelling training and fulfill the seemingly impossible demands of his strict dojo.

Out of the more than 100 students in his initial class, only seven lasted to the end. Mutassem was one of them, earning his 4th degree black belt at the age of 16. But he didn't stop there. Indeed, so fervently had he come to espouse karate's teachings, and so convinced was he of its positive influence in his life, that he felt compelled to share it with others, to instill in young people the values – the self-discipline, the respect for others, the faith in effort – that had served him so well in everything he did.

So, in May 2010, Mutassem partnered with his sensei, Mansoor al-Batrani, to co-find the Strive Karate Club in Muscat. Together, Mansoor and Mutassem coach students, or *karateka*, 6 years old and above with an emphasis on the development of character through physical training. 'To strive for the perfection of character; to follow the paths of truth; to foster a spirit of effort; to honour the principles of etiquette; and to guard against impetuous courage.' Such are the five core ethics of karate, and it's these, says Mutassem, more than mastery of the moves themselves, which guide training at every level.

A BOLD MOVE AND BOUNTEOUS REWARDS

Four years overseas had done Mutassem good. Far from home for the first time in his life, he'd learned to adapt to a new environment, to see the world with new eyes. By the time he graduated from Curtin, he had grown in ways he couldn't have anticipated, forging new friendships, expanding his horizons, and finding in himself a talent for leadership he never knew he possessed. Personally and professionally, spiritually and emotionally, Mutassem had matured; he knew what he wanted; he understood who he was.

And yet, upon his return to Oman, the way forward was anything but clear. During his last semester at Curtin, Mutassem had received a job offer from Oman's telecommunications regulatory authority. The agency was looking for an economist, and Mutassem needed to pay the bills. The salary was good. The hours were reasonable, and the alternatives were few. 'So I accepted it', he says.

Things went well enough for the first year. But Mutassem soon realised how much he was missing. 'I wasn't stimulated intellectually', he says. 'And I was too comfortable.' While many people would consider comfort a good thing, karate had taught Mutassem to avoid it, he says. 'Discomfort strengthens the spirit.' Anxious to find a way out, Mutassem spent every moment of his free time in self-reflection, searching his thoughts for what it was he should do with his life, and after filling several notebooks, he finally arrived at a realisation: 'that I needed to do more', he says. 'I wasn't going to occupy a space on this earth just to do a job that pays well.'

Still, leaving, he knew, would not be easy. 'In this part of the world, there is so much pressure to do what's normal', he says. 'So much authority telling you what to do and what not to do.' Nevertheless, Mutassem had made his decision; he would go his own way. 'I knew I wanted to become a motivational speaker and a writer', he says. 'I didn't know how I would do it; I just knew that I would.' Then, one day, he got a call from a friend: 'He asked me if I would give a workshop to university students.'

Seized by the doubt that he couldn't do it, Mutassem hesitated. 'I thought about how I didn't have much experience as a public speaker', he says. 'But then I remembered that for much of the past year, I had been telling myself I was one, and I knew that at some point, I had to walk the talk.' Adrenaline pumping, his voice shaky, Mutassem agreed to do the workshop, and that decision, he says, 'changed my life forever.'

Less than two years after leaving his government job, Mutassem has reached more than 1,000 people with his inspirational talks and training programmes. An accomplished writer, he's penned a number of articles for newspapers and magazines on personal and intellectual growth, and regularly updates a LinkedIn page with new insights. He's even begun working on his first novel.

But it's the Enriching Experience that demands most of Mutassem's time, and not least for its ever-increasing popularity. 'I think the idea of tolerance is not very strong in this part of the world', he says. 'People tend to have their views, and they usually aren't open to others, especially with regard to topics considered taboo, like faith and politics.' With the Enriching Experience, he says, Omanis have a forum in which they can speak freely, debate issues, and learn.

Mutassem has no illusions of replacing Facebook. But he does believe that in a world so saturated with social media, there is a growing awareness of the value of the kind of face-to-face interactions facilitated by the Enriching Experience. Given that social media is a global phenomenon, the Enriching Experience has the potential, he believes, to expand internationally. 'To every corner of the earth', he says. 'And to nurture learning in all spheres of knowledge: business, medicine, literature, history, psychology – anything.'

'My vision, my hope', he says, 'is that this will help encourage people to formulate their own opinions and to share those opinions.' It's especially important, he adds, 'that we start with young people. This can help lay the foundation for a more tolerant society.'

An unseen star of the Arab world, Mutassem al-Sharji made his way in the world on his own terms. Driven by a hunger for knowledge, and a desire to share it, he weathered the pressure to stay in a stable job, and instead, struck out on his own. Although the Enriching Experience may never achieve the world-spanning reach Mutassem envisions, its mere existence is a testament to the power of imagination and the impact one person can have.

Raghda El-Ebrashi

Alashanek Ya Balady

I HEARD IT FIRST FROM QUEEN RANIA OF JORDAN — THE amazing story of a 12-year-old Egyptian girl, a young woman from a well-to-do family, whose life was indelibly altered — transformed, even — by a chance encounter on a school trip.

The queen had referenced the story in a rousing speech to the class of 2010 at the American University in Cairo (AUC), her own alma mater. As the wide-eyed young graduates took their diplomas and headed out into the world, she wanted them to see that there is more to life than material possessions, to appreciate the value of volunteerism, and to find inspiration in civic engagement, which she called 'a quintessentially Arab idea.'

'There is no greater failure than having the potential to accomplish more yet settling for less', the Queen told the crowd, quoting the great 10th century poet, Al Mutannabi, amongst the finest in the Arabic language. 'Deeply rooted in our culture, for hundreds of years, is this principle of civic engagement. But, if you looked at the Arab world today, you'd be forgiven for asking what happened to this

principle. Too often, it seems our citizenship is spelled
with an 'S.' We *sit* still. We *sit* back. We *sit* on the sidelines.'

Social progress, she went on, is not a passive process.
'It doesn't come from governments looking down,
directing change. It comes from communities, families,
and individuals looking up, driving society forward, fuelled
by nothing more than an idea and an instinct to do good.
It comes from civic engagement.' There could hardly be
a better example of this, she said, than her fellow AUC
alumna, a young woman by the name of Raghda El-
Ebrashi, whose innovative outreach to Egypt's poor and
marginalised has been nothing short of remarkable.

It all began at a nursing home on the outskirts of Cairo.
Raghda, then a 5th grader with only the faintest idea of
life beyond the comfortable confines of her privileged
existence, was visiting the home with her classmates, an
activity organised by her school, when she happened upon
the cleaning lady. Clothed in threadbare garments, her back
bent from a lifetime of labour, the woman was as frail and
feeble, and it seemed to Raghda, as the home's elderly
residents. Om Fathi was her name, and she approached
Raghda with a warm smile, guessing that she must be the
same age as her own daughters. The two chatted for a few
minutes, and when it was time to leave, Om Fathy invited
Raghda to visit her home and to meet her children – all
seven of them.

'At that time, I didn't know that this was poverty',
Raghda would later recall. 'An entire family living in a 3
x 2 metre house. There wasn't even enough space for all of
the children to lay down, so they took turns sleeping.' It was
a side of Cairo she had never before seen, had never even
imagined. Raghda had always taken for granted her many

amenities, she says – the television, the car, the room to call her own. But during that first visit, Om Fathi asked her to list aloud her many blessings. 'After I finished, she told me, "there is something you have but you did not mention"', Raghda recalls. 'I said, "What is that, Om Fathi?" She said, "Look up and you will know." And it was only then that I realised that all of this time we had been standing under the night sky – that there was no ceiling over our heads.'

That was the moment, says Raghda, that her eyes were first opened – that she saw the world as it really was. Looking up at Om Fathi's ceiling of stars, she thought back to the way her teachers had always told her a house should be drawn: as a rectangle with small square windows and a triangle roof. 'They said that every house looks just so, and for the first time, I understood that this isn't true – that for many people, there is no triangle, there is not even a rectangle.'

Raghda's epiphany led her to examine her own life more closely, and to question many of her assumptions about the world, the things she always thought she knew. For example, she says, 'We were also told that everyone graduates from university, and then everyone gets a job.' But Om Fathi's children, even the youngest of them, had never been to school, Raghda says ruefully. 'They had to work instead.'

Raghda decided, then, that she had had enough. If what she had learned from Om Fathi was true, then her teachers had been wrong. They had misled her. She wouldn't waste another minute sitting in their classrooms. 'I told my parents, I don't want to go to school anymore because what they tell me is bad information.' Her parents pleaded with her to change her mind, but Raghda persisted. Back and forth, they went, until finally, her parents proposed a deal: 'They said, OK, if you will go to school, we will send you to Om Fathi every week.'

So it was: during the week, Raghda attended her usual classes. But come Friday, she would take the bus across town for extra-curricular instruction with Om Fathi. She played with the kids, taught them to sing and dance, and talked for hours on end with the wise old woman. As the weeks turned into months, the two grew closer and closer, becoming like family, and Raghda's enthusiasm for the visits never flagged. While her classmates were content not to stray from their sheltered lives, pleasantly insulated, as they were, from the daily stresses of the poor, Raghda was seeking out the real world, the unvarnished truth.

Indeed, Raghda dared to be different. If at first they were confounded by it all, Raghda's parents soon realised that it was through helping people that their daughter found happiness. With that in mind, they lent her their full support, urging her to follow her passion wherever it might take her.

FORGING A PATH

By the time she arrived at AUC, Raghda was steeped in experience. Having seen firsthand how Egypt's poor struggle to make ends meet, she had spent her high school years volunteering with NGOs, doing whatever she could to help the many other families like Om Fathi's. It was noble work, and necessary, and as Raghda entered university, she looked forward to meeting young people who shared her passion and energy, students as committed as she to aiding the country's less fortunate.

But Raghda would be disappointed by what she found.

Far from feeling sympathy for Egyptians of more modest means, most of her fellow classmates seemed to look on them with disdain, preferring to keep their distance. The few that did try to reach out did so only by donating money or material goods. Although it was well-intentioned, Raghda knew that charity alone could never address the problem at its root — the rampant unemployment and yawning inequality that keeps so many Egyptians mired in poverty with no means of escape.

Indeed, it was just as Om Fathi had told her the day before she died. As the weak old woman lay sick in bed, Raghda seated by her side, she whispered a final request — that Raghda continue to work with the people of her community and that she always remember what Om Fathi had taught her. It's one thing to give money or food, she had said. These are acts of kindness no one can criticise. But in order to truly help those in need, to have a lasting impact on people's lives, goodwill isn't enough. One has to engage with communities in need. To do that, a person has to cultivate in him or herself that most noble of human sentiments: solidarity. This, Om Fathi had said, is the difficult first step, and one few people ever manage to take.

Raghda herself, of course, was amongst those few. But how to persuade others to follow her lead? How to counter the prejudices so prevalent in Egyptian society? And how to convince those accustomed to pity-driven charity to embrace instead a more sustainable form of civic engagement? The challenge consumed her. For weeks, Raghda racked her brain and came up with nothing. Then one day her jumbled thoughts crystallised into a simple thesis: If every able-bodied citizen believed in his or her ability to help the less fortunate and acted on it, there would be no one left living in poverty, no one without proper healthcare or enough food to eat.

Raghda decided that rather than urge her fellow classmates to become change agents for the poor, she would establish a student club and invite them to join. Thus was born Alashanek Ya Balady (AYB), or for 'For My Country'. A pioneering approach to poverty alleviation, AYB was designed to break down the sturdy walls separating Egypt's haves and have-nots. Through direct engagement with marginalised communities, AYB volunteers endeavoured to equip underprivileged youth with market-relevant skills – to fill the gap between the outputs of Egypt's failing education system and the vastly different demands of the labour market.

While at first it was met with scepticism, AYB quickly grew in popularity, attracting the many students who had craved an opportunity to make a difference. In a matter of months, Raghda's dream had become reality; AYB had blazed a new path, becoming the university's first developmental student club, and engendered in students a spirit of civic responsibility that spread first throughout the university and then far beyond its borders. Indeed, after two years in operation, AYB had been franchised to universities across Egypt, and in 2005, Raghda registered the club as a non-governmental organisation (NGO), putting the model she had forged out there for all to see – and more importantly, for all to embrace as their own.

Yet, she soon decided that this model needed to be refined. If AYB was to have a meaningful impact, it wasn't enough to simply train underprivileged youth. For one, Egypt's deep class divisions ensured that prospective employers would not just happen upon young people from low-income areas, or vice versa. Moreover, in the event that marginalised youth did manage to secure an interview, they would likely be judged, she knew, not on their fitness for the job but on where they're from. Stereotyped as dishonest and incompetent, poor youth would never get a fair shot at the best jobs, no matter how qualified for a position they might be.

'We all know the old Chinese proverb', says Raghda: '*Give a man a fish; you feed him for a day. Teach a man to fish; you feed him for a lifetime.*' But what if the fishing industry is rigged to favour the rich? What if a monopoly on fish markets keeps prices so low that the fisherman can't feed his family? And what if the fisherman, who doesn't have the same rights as other workers, gets injured on the job? What good is his fishing knowledge then? That line of inquiry led Raghda to the conclusion that in simply training youth, she had left too much to chance. AYB, she decided, would have to modify its approach, to target both sides of the equation.

In the weeks that followed, Raghda and her team of volunteers began working to identify companies' precise needs, and actively searching for vacancies, becoming in effect a veritable employment agency. In 2008, the NGO signed its first contract with a company in Cairo; for a fee, AYB would select, train, and mentor youth for sales and customer service positions; and the work didn't stop there. After a youth had been hired, AYB would monitor his or her progress over the first three months, provide life skills coaching, and work with management to ensure that the new hire was paid a fair wage, provided decent working conditions, and protected by labour laws.

In the years since, AYB has continued to evolve, adding new partners and launching new projects, and all the while remaining faithful to its core mission. In 2012, for example, AYB launched Egypt@Work, which provided underprivileged youth, both men and women, with microloans to start small businesses. Funded by the MasterCard Foundation in partnership with the International Youth Federation and the NGO Nahdet El Mahrousa, the programme assisted thousands of beneficiaries in generating their own income and even creating employment opportunities for others. Another microfinance project, started the same year with support from the JP Morgan Chase Foundation, helped close to 300 more beneficiaries and their families in Cairo and Upper Egypt secure a stable source of income and a dignified living.

One of AYB's most ambitious undertakings to date is the Comprehensive Family Development Project. First launched in Alexandria with support from ExxonMobile Egypt, the project targeted 10 families in an impoverished area of the city called 'Al Haramein', providing each with a set of three services, including skills training and microloans for the family's breadwinners; courses designed to nurture children's creative potential and strengthen their communication and leadership skills; and health and personal hygiene education for all. Based on that project's success, and in partnership with the Bank of Alexandria, it was later replicated in a similar section of Cairo called Ain El Seera, helping to lift 10 additional families out of poverty there.

In an effort to assist those who fall through the cracks, those who, whether because of health problems or obligations to family, are unable to find work in the formal sector, AYB also provides vocational training. Two projects funded by the Dutch and Japanese embassies, for example, trained beneficiaries in skills like carpentry, sewing and tailoring, poultry raising, meat packing and iron welding – all of them integral to various vibrant industries, and thus perpetually in high demand.

In a similar vein, and in partnership with the Cairo-based company Schaduf, AYB has helped struggling families turn to rooftop farming, an eco-friendly and increasingly popular form of agriculture(AYB provides families with the seeds free of charge, and Schaduf sells the produce on the open market, putting the proceeds toward AYB's loans). AYB has even released its own line of stylish notebooks. Designed by its social venture and sister company Tafanin for Arts & Design, the notebooks are sold in 'On the Run' stores, and a portion of the profits is reinvested in AYB activities.

Yet, what most distinguishes AYB from anything in the region – and what endows it, I believe, with truly transformative potential – is the replicable nature of its work. 'I think if you ask social entrepreneurs about their goals, most would tell you that they want to grow their organisation, to extend its reach farther and farther', says Raghda. While that can be a very good thing, she adds, AYB aspires to do something different. 'We do not care if AYB is the biggest or the most popular organisation in Egypt', she says. 'What we want is for this sustainable model of development to be widely replicated. We think it can have an impact, not only in alleviating poverty, but in spreading this idea that we all have a responsibility to our fellow citizens, and that's why we've franchised it to other NGOs under their name, not under our own.'

A QUIET LEADER

When I first met Raghda on a visit to Cairo, I must say I could barely hide my surprise. It was just so hard to believe that someone so young could be so self-possessed, so poised, so certain of the way forward – and yet so pleasingly free of the hubris that often accompanies great success. For all of the recognition she's received – from the King Abdullah II Award for Youth Innovation and Achievement and a '35 Under 35' award given out by World Business Magazine and Shell International to a fellowship with Ashoka, the global platform for social entrepreneurship – Raghda has kept her feet firmly planted on the ground.

Indeed, as loud a voice as she is for Egypt's marginalised youth, Raghda herself shuns the spotlight; she is soft-spoken, evidently allergic to self-promotion, and quick to credit colleagues for what AYB has managed to achieve. 'There are many people who helped me along the way, many volunteers who implemented the plan, who actually put it into action', she says; and were it not for her parent's support, Raghda says she would never have come to know her late friend and mentor, Om Fathi, who set the whole thing in motion. 'They believed in me so much. They encouraged me to take risks, and they made sure I received the best education I could get.'

Reflecting on the state of social enterprise in Egypt, Raghda added that it really isn't important that the world knows of her virtues. In fact, all too often in Egypt, she says, the social entrepreneur becomes the subject of conversation; his or her selflessness or kindness or humility is thought to be what makes the business tick, the animating spirit that keeps the whole thing afloat. 'We have this flawed assumption that the leader is more important than the organisation, and that without this person, the rest of it can't survive.' But that isn't true, she says, recalling a difficult period in the past, when several of AYB's biggest donors were denied approval by the government. To keep the projects going, 50 members of her staff had to go without a salary for six months. Raghda became depressed and weak, and to compound her woes, one of her closest friends suddenly passed away.

'My colleagues, my friends, they were there for me', she says. 'And they always are. When I'm feeling weak or pessimistic, they give me their smiles, they pray for me, and we take the next step.'

As AYB's chairperson, Raghda takes no salary, which is why most days you can find her presiding over classes at the German University of Cairo, where she is a professor of marketing. Raghda teaches her students how to blend business with social good, how to make a profit and a difference, and whenever she has the chance, she takes them into the field for the same sort of exposure that first sparked her own passion for civic engagement. 'We have to educate people not only on the concept, but also the practice', she says, adding that it would be best to plant this seed as early as possible, by making it part of the primary school or high school curriculum.

Chatting there in her office at GUC, I asked Raghda about her ambitions. Where would she go from here? What did she hope to achieve? She paused for a moment, and then said, 'I'd like to one day become a minister of social affairs'. Raghda explained matter-of-factly that such a position would allow her to reach all of the 80 million people in Egypt. 'I don't want to see anyone in this country who is needy or poor or without dignity'. But as I sat there listening to her speak so articulately about youth unemployment and the urgent need to address it, I couldn't help but wonder to myself if she might someday occupy an even higher office.

No one told Raghda El-Ebrashi how to be a leader. It was her determination to do more for the poor and marginalised that led her to a cause far larger than herself. In AYB, Raghda has created an organisation like none before it, a paradigm-shifting innovation with untold potential for good. Undaunted by the prospect of failure, she forged ahead, won followers, and found success.

Safiya al-Bahlani

An Artist's Evolution

FOR THE FIRST THREE YEARS OF HER LIFE, SAFIYA AL-Bahlani called the hospital her home. Born with a congenital disorder called phocomelia, she entered the world in a physical condition few people are forced to endure from the start: no forearms, a deformed knee, and a deformed foot. She was also deaf in her right ear.

But to describe Safiya as 'disabled' would be a serious mischaracterisation. For, if life robbed her of certain physical abilities, it also endowed her with exceptional talent, and it's for this that the 25-year-old artist has become something of a celebrity in her native Oman. Indeed, far from 'disabled', Safiya now stands tall – living proof of the power of perseverance, of the idea that no challenge is too great, and that the only thing stopping any of us from achieving our goals is not believing that we can.

I must say, though, what impressed me most about Safiya when I finally had the chance to meet her was something less easily put to paper – her presence, a calm, measured poise, a seemingly unshakable self-assurance. Even before she had shared with me her remarkable story, it was plainly evident that in overcoming her physical deficits, Safiya had developed a sturdiness of character seldom seen in someone so young. Among the many unseen stars of the Arab world, this one, I thought to myself – she may just shine the brightest.

It all started, Safiya told me, with a circle. The first face she drew was little more than that. Featureless, but for the eyes. In time, they became ovals, with ears and noses, mouths and chins, and from there she progressed to portraits – full bodies with arms and legs, people seated and standing. Each picture was better than the last, her pencil work improving with every draft, and with that, her confidence growing as well. But one body part Safiya could never bring herself to sketch was a hand. 'My images were always a mirror of myself', she once told TEDx audience at Institut Le Rosey. 'Hands weren't me.'

When we met in Muscat last March, Safiya was just back from Doha, where she had recently wrapped up a prestigious art residency with the British Council Qatar. Two of the paintings she had been commissioned to do there were to be featured later that month in the ILHAM Art Exhibition at Doha's Museum of Islamic Art, a marvelous I.M. Pei-designed space set on Doha Harbour, itself a monument to Islamic heritage, and Safiya was still buzzing from the experience. 'It was a whole group of artists who are successful and are challenged in various ways', she said. 'It was like, you know, *wow, this is home.*'

Held under the patronage of Her Excellency Sheikha Al Mayassa bint Hamad bin Khalifa Al-Thani, the chairperson of Qatar Museums, the ILHAM Exhibition showcased new works by physically-challenged artists from Qatar, Oman and the UK to conclude a four-day conference organised by the British Council. Part of the British Council's 'Definitely Able' initiative, the event brought together international and local stakeholders to address the many barriers that continue to prevent people with disabilities from full participating in society — everything from legislation and learning technologies to societal attitudes, employability, and access to education. Through art and dialogue, the conference sought to 'challenge perceptions about disability', while also highlighting best practices for making communities more inclusive and creating opportunities for people of all talents.

It was an honour, Safiya said, to have her work given such an important platform.

But more than that, the event had changed her outlook — her perceptions, both of who she is and what she wants to accomplish. You see, for so long, she explained, 'It was about proving that I'm capable, that I have these skills, that society should accept me.' Also, that was no easy thing, especially as a child; classmates teased her and called her names. Teachers told her that it was best she didn't participate in group activities — swimming or dance lessons or even school itself — because the other kids might be scared of her.

The stares, the snickers, the silent judgements: they were constant and unrelenting, and Safiya dealt with it all, the only way she knew how. If she was to fit in with her classmates, if she was ever to be 'normal' in the eyes of society, she knew she would have to hide who she is. 'I never talked about my challenges', she said, 'Because I thought that exposing them would be a form of weakness.' At that time in her life, weakness wasn't really an option. Kids can be cruel, Safiya knew, so she would have to be strong. But just how strong she would become, Safiya couldn't imagine.

By leaving her physically dependent, phocomelia had made her almost preternaturally tough – able to rise above even the harshest of insults without batting an eye. She had always been shy and soft-spoken. But emotionally, Safiya was mature beyond her years, and far ahead of her peers. 'It did hurt initially', she recalled. 'But those moments that make you feel low, they give you the motivation to keep going', she said. 'Challenge is your weapon.'

Indeed, far from holding her back, Safiya's challenges fuelled her forward movement. From a young age, she set out to prove that even without hands, she could create beautiful works of art, and between exhibitions of her work at Bank Muscat, the U.S. Embassy in Oman, Doha's Museum of Islamic Art, and elsewhere, Safiya has proved that beyond a doubt.

As a result, she said, 'I no longer have to hide who I am'. Having proven herself as an artist, she wanted to approach art anew: whereas before, painting and drawing had been her outlet, a cathartic exercise through which she could give vent to her daily struggle for acceptance, Safiya had come to see it as an opportunity – a means of advocating on behalf not only of herself but of others like her. 'I want to use my art and my standing to support a political movement for people with challenges', she said. 'I want to push them to speak out about it, because why should we hide who we are?'

CHALLENGE IS YOUR WEAPON

I want to be a painter so I can express myself through my paintings.
I want to be able to paint wide oceans that go as far as my sight can

see. I want to be able to paint forests that are filled with lavishing
trees and colourful scented flowers.

Safiya was in the third grade when she penned these lines
expressing her aspiration to become an artist. She had at
first been fascinated by faces, she told me – their mystery
and meaning, the stories embedded in every feature, every
wrinkle of the flesh. Yet with each attempt to reproduce
on paper the faces she saw in person, Safiya always felt she
had come up short. As hard as she tried, she could never
meet her own high standards, the flawlessness she had come
to expect of herself.

Frustrated by what she saw as failure, Safiya moved
on to landscapes. Creative, and resourceful, she not only
overcame her physical challenges – she used them to her
advantage, developing a style all her own, a way of painting
no able-bodied artist could ever perfectly replicate. At first,
of course, she struggled. In art class, when the teacher
instructed the students to use their paper and scissors to
create a picture, Safiya was at a loss. 'I thought, how am I
going to create something with scissors? I can't even cut
a straight line!'

'I hated it', she said. 'It took me *forever*. Every student
had finished, and was already gone, and still I was sitting
there at my desk, trying to complete the assignment.' Then,
one day, she had an idea. After the rest of the students
had finished, Safiya went around the room and picked up
the scraps of paper they had left scattered on the floor.
The teacher had encouraged her to create something that
spoke to her heritage, to her roots in Oman, and so, with
those discarded cuttings, she fashioned a scene of Muscat
at dusk – mosques and palm trees silhouetted against the
sky. As anyone who has seen it can attest, the results were

nothing short of brilliant. 'I always found a way', she said. 'Nothing stopped me.'

By this point, Safiya had become so accustomed to confronting challenges in every sphere of life that she began to seek them out. 'As an artist, I always looked for the hardest thing I could do', she said. 'I always wanted to push myself.' Like a track star training for the decathlon, Safiya forced herself to hone a variety of skills rather than practice, over and over, her one or two best. 'As a child, I wanted to be many things: a police officer, a doctor, a teacher', she said, and though her ambitions changed with age, her capacity to imagine a new reality never diminished. Even after learning of her gift for painting and drawing, she says, 'I began to seriously contemplate what else I could do with my creative talents.'

As a high school senior, Safiya might have coasted to graduation. But her art teacher, who knew she had great potential, urged her to take college-level classes; and even in those, she excelled. Still, by the time she graduated, Safiya felt she still didn't fully understand many of the fundamentals of drawing – where to position objects, how to realistically render light and shadow and the textures of nature. So she taught herself.

'I started watching lessons on YouTube', she said. 'And every day, I did sketch after sketch after sketch.' It also occurred to Safiya that she had never been properly introduced to oil painting. Though she had tried her hand at it in the past, she could never keep the colours from mixing. Instead of reverting to what she knew, she went to another artist, an expert in oils, and asked for her help. 'And at last, I learned', she said. 'You have to wait for each layer to dry before applying the next. That taught me patience. It took me almost two months to paint my first piece, but I did it.'

In confronting new challenges, Safiya also faced down her fears, including her greatest fear of all: people. Throughout her life, people had judged her, laughed at her, told her she shouldn't or couldn't. When she was at her lowest, Safiya would turn for comfort to her stuffed animals, and especially her Barbie dolls, 'because they looked most like real people.' Dressing them up in different outfits, she would have them act out the activities she wasn't allowed to do herself – the swim lessons, the ballet – and imagine a life with all of her limbs just so, uncomplicated by an outward appearance that caused others discomfort.

'So I took on portraits', she said, and realising she was rather good at this – friends around town began queuing up for their own – she decided to keep at it. It was through portraiture, she says, that another challenge resurfaced: painting hands and fingers. 'I had always thought to myself, if I don't have them, why should I draw them?' Safiya started with a photo she'd recently come across – that of a fisherman's leathery, weatherworn hands. 'Every line was telling me, *Stop, you can't do this.*' But, yes, she did that too, and then she did more.

She went to Jordan to learn graphic design and animation, challenging for the use of math it required. During a trip to Tanzania, she came across street artists who could quickly sketch a scene before them in the moments before it vanished. Safiya saw in this another challenge, another opportunity. 'Because I'm slow as an artist, I decided have to be quick. So every afternoon, I sat on the patio, and sketched whatever came by as quickly as I could.'

Back in Oman, Safiya had only ever drawn things that were big, she explained. So why not try something detailed? Some kind of intricate pattern. She focused her efforts on henna, and created designs based on calligraphy and the letters of the Arabic alphabet. Here again, Safiya was a quick study. 'I used to trace my mom's hand', she said, and with a laugh, added, 'I guess you could say she "lent me a hand."'

A MOTHER, A PARTNER, A FRIEND

Long before she had ever met her daughter, Dr Sabah al-Bahlani, CEO of the Association of Early Intervention for Children with Disabilities and founding director of Health Education and Information in Oman's Ministry of Health, had developed a passion for helping people who couldn't help themselves. In fact, she was only five years old when she started down that path in the Kenyan village where she grew up.

'My mother and my aunt told me that I used to collect all the children in the neighbourhood and take them to the common place where people bathe', she recalled in a recent Tedx event held at the beautiful Bait Al Zubair Museum, a jewel of Muscat's old town. 'I would ask them to take a bath, and I supervised them.' Years later, while living in an apartment her family shared with other relatives, Sabah realised her 2-year-old cousin couldn't walk. 'At 4 o'clock, all of us would go to play on the playground, and she couldn't do that', she said. 'So, I decided to carry her every day to the playground, and I taught her to walk.'

When Sabah moved to Oman as a young girl in the early Sixties, the country had little in the way of modern health care. With fewer than five hospitals serving the entire country, and all of those concentrated in the major cities, Omanis living in rural areas often went without care altogether, their short lives made painful and brief by the maladies attendant to poverty. It was only on visits to the city, often several days' journey by foot, that they might come across a doctor or a nurse – or someone like Sabah, who provided what care she could out of the kindness of her heart.

'Our family from Izki used to come visit us in Muscat', she said, 'and I realised that many of these people, especially the kids, they had trachoma.' An infection of the eyes that can result in blindness, trachoma most often occurs in poor, rural communities with limited access to clean water and health care. 'Their eyes were closed', she said, describing how the lashes turn in and scrape the cornea. 'So, I asked my father to buy me a first aid kit, and everyone who came, I started treating them. But my father didn't think that was appropriate.'

Upon graduating from high school, Sabah had dreams of becoming a doctor. She wanted to go to America to study medicine, and though her family opposed it – people didn't think it was a good idea for a woman to practice medicine, she said – Sabah went anyway. It was in America that Sabah realised she could have a greater impact in Oman by studying community health education. Rather than work one-on-one with patients, she would work to educate communities about how to care for themselves, and when she returned to Oman, that's exactly what she did.

'For two years, I was going to villages in remote areas, in the mountains', she said. At one village, Sabah sat down with a woman in her home to give her health information.

As she talked, she noticed movement under a blanket on the floor. 'I thought, my God, what's that?' The woman told Sabah to ignore the blanket, but when it moved again, Sabah couldn't help herself. 'I went to lift it, and the mother said, No, no, don't touch it!' Underneath lay a disabled child. 'She was ashamed about her child and was trying to cover it', said Sabah. 'I thought that was bad.

That child deserved to be known and seen, to be part of the society. And since that day I decided I was going to work and speak for people with disabilities.'

Years later, a friend invited Sabah to work with her at a new women's association in Muscat that supported parents of children with disabilities. Sabah's job was to help parents communicate with their children. Once a week, they would gather together in a group and work on communication between mother and child. It was there that she first met a little girl named Safiya.

'One of my first memories before the adoption was when my mother invited me to an Eid gathering with her family', Safiya said. It was one of the rare occasions when she was allowed to leave the hospital, and she hoped the day would never end. When it did, Sabah took her back to the hospital, where she was met with several angry nurses. 'They thought I made their job harder because Safiya didn't want to go back to her bed in the hospital', Sabah recalled. 'So I went to the Ministry and I said I don't think this is right. Kids like Safiya need to be out, participating in society, not in the hospital, and they said, 'No one wanted to take Safiya out of the hospital. If you will take her, we will give her to you.'

'I was shocked', said Sabah, her voice shaking. 'Within one week, I was able to adopt Safiya.'

Ever since then, the pair has made the journey through life side-by-side, supporting one another every step of the way. 'Every kid, when they get frustrated with a drawing, they throw it in the garbage', said Safiya. 'I was no different. But I had a mom who saw potential in me since I was small.' Every drawing Safiya discarded, Sabah would put in a folder. 'And now, looking through them, I can see how much I've grown and learned', said Safiya. 'How far I've come.'

'She's been a lifelong source of support, and she was advocating on my behalf even before I came into her life', Safiya says of her mother. 'And now I'm learning to become an advocate for others – to speak up for those who don't know how.'

Never one to settle for mediocrity, Safiya al-Bahlani became the artist she is today by always holding herself to the same standard as her more able-bodied peers. A victim she is not. Relentless in her quest for perfection, she is a model of perseverance and resolve, and her achievements – as an artist and as an individual – should inspire us all to reach for excellence.

Sarah Hermez
Creative Space Beirut

TAKING A CHANCE

FOR SARAH HERMEZ, FOUNDING DIRECTOR OF CREATIVE Space Beirut, the light bulb moment came over coffee in New York, just a few blocks from her alma mater, the New School for Public Engagement, Visual & Performing Arts, where she had double-majored in fashion design and media studies.

It was early November 2010. A year earlier, the young Lebanese designer had made the bold decision to leave the comforts of midtown Manhattan, and the many job opportunities that awaited her there, for a far less certain future in Beirut.

Born and raised in Kuwait, Sarah had been to Lebanon many times to visit relatives, and she had stayed for one six-month stretch in 2003 during the U.S.-Iraq War. 'But I had never actually lived there', she says. 'I'd been living in New York for seven years, and I was carrying around a passport that said I was Lebanese – but I didn't really understand what that meant.' So, in what she cites as one of two pivotal moments in her life, she decided to go, eventually finding work in the textiles department of a furniture company, as well as with the non-profit Unite Lebanon Youth Project, teaching Palestinian children from the city's refugee camps.

Taking that courageous step to start from scratch in a new city had paid off. Though she hardly knew anyone in Beirut, Sarah had found ways to pursue the things she most loved – creativity and social justice – all the while reconnecting with her roots; originally from Adana, Turkey, her grandfather, who is Assyrian, had grown up an orphan, mostly in Lebanon. He later moved to Palestine, where he met Sarah's grandmother, an Armenian then living in Jerusalem, and the two later permanently resettled in Beirut – 'and that's how we became Lebanese', she says.

Still, things weren't quite right. As much as she enjoyed what she was doing, Sarah hadn't figured out how to fuse her dual passions, and she knew she wouldn't be content until she did. So she turned for advice to her friend and longtime mentor, Caroline Shlala-Simonelli. A professor at the New School's Parsons School of Design and, at 74, a wise veteran of the fashion industry, Caroline too traced her roots to Lebanon; though her parents had emigrated to the United States during the first world war, Caroline had been brought up in a Lebanese household and understood Arabic. However, unlike Sarah, she had never visited.

'We were at the Dean & Deluca on 39th street, and I was explaining to Caroline this problem I was having – that I couldn't figure out how to combine these two separate lives I was living in Beirut.' During her time at Parsons – a rigorous 4-year programme – Sarah had come to regard creativity, she says, as vital to her very being. A career in fashion design, she knew, could give her the creative outlet she needed. But fashion for the sake of fashion wasn't what she had in mind. 'I knew that I wasn't interested in making clothes for rich people. That just didn't make sense to me.'

If Sarah's career goals differed from those of her peers at Parsons, so too did her experiences as an undergraduate. Indeed, even as she honed her technical skills and deepened her knowledge of fashion design, Sarah pursued a degree in media and culture studies at the New School's Eugene Lang College of Liberal Arts. At Lang, she enrolled in study abroad programmes that would take her to places far from the classroom and equally far from her comfort zone, putting her face-to-face with a reality, few in the West ever see.

First, she travelled to Dharamsala, India, home of the Dalai Lama, to study Tibetan politics. 'I lived with a family of Tibetan refugees and learned all about their cause and what they've endured for their beliefs', she recalls. 'That was eye-opening'. Later, she ventured to Siem Reap to study Cambodian politics, and worked in an orphanage in the city as part of a programme that emphasised experiential learning. There, she witnessed a country struggling to heal the wounds of war and dictatorship, a land rich in natural resources, yet mired in poverty.

'Those experiences together radically changed the way I viewed the world and my engagement with it', she says. 'And I began asking myself what it was I really wanted to do.'

That morning at the café, Sarah was talking and talking, she says, while Caroline sat there silently, listening as she described her situation, sipping her coffee, nodding now and then in agreement. 'And then all of a sudden Caroline looked at me and said, "Sarah, why don't you start a free school for fashion design?" And I said, Yes! Yes, why don't

I?! That's exactly what I want to do! And then I looked at her and said, "Caroline, will you come and help me?" She said, "Of course I'll come, just make it happen". And that's how this whole thing began.'

Also at the café that day was a close friend who was working for Donna Karan New York, one of the world's leading fashion houses. 'She told me, if you do this, I'll donate $100,000 worth of fabric', Sarah recalls. 'So right away, I had an experienced business partner in Caroline, and I had all the fabric I would need to get started. Now I needed the school.'

There was just one problem, she says. 'I had no idea how to start a non-profit, much less a non-profit school.' Reflecting on that moment at a TEDx event in Beirut, Sarah recalled the mixture of excitement and trepidation she felt as she set about the task: 'I had never been a leader before', she told the audience. 'I was very comfortable following people I respected, but I was never a mentor. And I just remembered what Caroline had told me – she said, "a leader is made when a leader is needed"...and I guess it was needed.'

Wasting no time, Sarah returned to Beirut to write up a funding proposal for the new project. For the first time in her life, she knew exactly where she was going. She had a vision, a purpose, a plan. But how to get to her destination, how to turn that vision into reality – that would be another matter altogether.

A FREE SCHOOL

When I first heard about Creative Space Beirut, I myself didn't fully understand what the organisation was or what exactly it aimed to accomplish. Fashion, I have to admit, has never been a particular passion of mine, and so, news of a free school for fashion design didn't initially grab my attention.

But the more I learned about Sarah, the more impressed I became with her courage and determination, and I soon realised that the problem she was addressing – an issue, essentially, of inequality – had implications far beyond the world of fashion. 'Design is the process by which we shape and structure our world', she explained. 'Not just the clothes that we wear, but the buildings we live in, the products we use.' If design is to promote social progress, she went on, it has to be inclusive, something that incorporates 'the voices and visions of people from all backgrounds.'

However, she says, when it comes to fashion, the poor don't get to participate. 'The industry is reserved for the elite', she says, explaining that most fashion design schools operate not as centres of learning and mentorship, but as businesses. 'They're for people who have money, people who can pay $50,000 dollars a year for an education, which is completely beyond the reach of the average young person.' Even at that price, she adds, students today don't get the kind of education they once did.

'Before design was institutionalised and privatised, people would work under mentorship. They would apprentice with designers, and they would learn the technical skills through the creative process.' Today's universities have divorced the two, she says, separating each skill into disparate classes – the drawing class, the draping class, the concepts class, and so on. 'We rejected this model for a more interdisciplinary approach, where the technical skill is embedded in the creative process, because at Creative Space Beirut, we believe that's what design is.'

Shortly after her conversation with Caroline, Sarah decided that the best thing to do would be to find an NGO interested in supporting her project. 'I thought an NGO would fund the whole thing, so I should take the proposal to one in Beirut', she recalls. 'And that's exactly what I did.' Within a few short days, the NGO she had approached replied to her request. 'They loved it', she says. 'I was so happy, I was over the moon. I thought, this is great, they'll provide the space and the money, and they'll find the students. Wonderful.'

As Sarah soon learned, though, that NGO support came with strings firmly attached. 'After a few months, I realised they were changing the objectives', she says. 'My plan was to teach five students over several years, but they wanted 50 students in the span of three weeks. They were more interested in quantity over quality, and they wanted a project with a start and an end. And that just wasn't what we had set out to do – so I decided against working with an NGO.' Forced to find another way, Sarah went back to the drawing board. She consulted Caroline, and then she turned to her father.

'He said he would fund a pilot project for three months', she says. 'So he gave us a deadline; by the end of that three months, Caroline and I would have to teach five students how to make dresses, and we would have to have made 30 dresses – enough to hold an exhibition and to generate sufficient income to continue. We had to demonstrate that this crazy idea, this free school, could actually work. That was the deal.'

With her seed funding in hand, Sarah's next task was to find a place to set up shop. For weeks, she looked and looked, finally coming upon a cave-like space underneath an Arabic School in a part of town called Achrafieh. 'It was really humid and dusty, but it was charming too in a way, and I thought, OK, this will do.' Then came the biggest challenge of all: finding the students. 'That was the hardest part', she says. 'I didn't know anyone in Lebanon.'

Sarah scoured the city for would-be designers – young men and women who aspired for a career in fashion but couldn't afford tuition at any of the country's other schools. 'I went all over knocking on doors – at women's centres, in the Palestinian refugee camps, at the offices of NGOs – and it was tough. Everyone liked the idea, but they wanted it in their own community.' In time, though, word of the new free fashion school got around, and the applications started coming in. 'I like to see portfolios', she says. 'I want to know that the applicant is creative and that whatever it is – artwork or fashion drawings – that it's self-taught and raw, and that it comes from passion.'

Caroline arrived in Beirut in June, and the pair officially launched the school that month. It was the start of a thrilling journey and a daunting challenge. 'We had three months to pull this off', Sarah recalls, 'and I kept asking myself: how in the world are we going to do it?' As it turned out, the first step was far easier than either of them had anticipated. 'We had all of this donated fabric from Donna Karan, and it occurred to us that we could just give it to the students and see what happens. So we said, OK, let's go for it!'

The results amazed them: 'Without having been taught any technical skills, without any real guidance, the students started to drape and to sculpt and to create', she says. 'And we realised then how much talent there was, and how much talent was being wasted – that the world was really missing out.' It was at that point, Sarah says, that she and Caroline instituted their 'progressive model' – the ages-old interdisciplinary approach to teaching design long since abandoned by today's universities.

The students – five in all – would arrive at 8:00 in the morning and work for 7 hours. They did this every day, week after week, and by the time the three months had come to an end, they had reached their target of 30 dresses. 'The students came together and worked very hard;, says Sarah. 'They learned from one another, and they motivated one another.' Days later, they threw a fundraising party and put the dresses on sale. 'And the turnout was incredible', she says. 'There were more than 300 people, and we sold every single piece. We generated more than $17,000 dollars, and that allowed us to continue. We proved it could work.'

BREAKING DOWN BARRIERS

Sarah's mother and father left Lebanon for Kuwait in 1974, just months before the start of the country's bloody, 15–year civil war. That conflict would turn a once beautiful Beirut into a bullet-scarred battleground, resulting in an estimated 120,000 fatalities and in the mass exodus of more than a million civilians. Not until 1989 did the fighting finally come to an end. But as in much of the MENA region, sectarian tensions remain to this day.

Those tensions mean that people of different backgrounds seldom mix, says Sarah. 'Communities are so divided that there are very few opportunities to be in the same room', she says. 'And if people don't have a reason to cross paths, they probably won't.' That lack of interaction, she says, inhibits dialogue, reinforcing the religious stereotypes that keep communities apart. Free education, she believes, can help bring people together. 'Lebanon is a very sectarian country', she says. 'You have these stark social and economic divisions. But free education can break down those walls and help us move forward together.'

Sarah has seen the proof of that in her own students. 'We currently have a class of 10, and they all come from very different households', she says. 'And what has happened, over time, is they've become a kind of family. They've realised that once you get under the surface, and once you get to know someone, deep down we're not so different. And that's been a wonderful thing to watch.'

Of course, she says, getting to where they are today was no cakewalk. 'The last four years were full of challenges – one after another after another.' First it was the funding. Then finding the students. Then, after they were up and running, Sarah and Caroline encountered a 'strange mentality' among the Lebanese elite, who seemed to shun Lebanese labels. 'It's as though you have to get a Western stamp of approval before you're accepted here', Sarah sighs. 'Which is why we decided to hold our first exhibition in Kuwait.'

With Creative Space Beirut, Sarah and Caroline had gone against the grain. They had boldly defied the status quo – the notion that fashion design is only for the privileged few, those with money and connections – and they had done it largely on their own, and if, for many, they were merely a curiosity – a kind of experiment in entrepreneurship – their reputation has steadily risen. After all, CSB's student designers have exhibited their work at some of the country's most prestigious venues – places like Saifi Urban Gardens, the Beirut Art centre, 6:05

Depechemode and the Bokja Design Studio – and even internationally at Kuwait's Contemporary Art Platform.

Sarah is quick to credit their many partners, including Parsons, which continues to send faculty members to CSB to serve as guest teachers, and the world-renowned designers – Donna Karan, Derek Lam, Diane Von Furstenberg – who've supported CSB with generous donations of high quality textiles.

Although she laments that her role has changed from creating to business planning, Sarah has steered the organisation to success; over the past three years, sales of student-produced dresses have generated more than $100,000 in revenue, all of which was later reinvested into CSB. To supplement that income, and subsidise her students' education, Sarah hopes to build Creative Space Beirut into its own brand. 'The way we operate today, students work all year on their individual collections, and at the end of the year, we sell the designs', she says. 'But now we're developing ready-to-wear products that we can sell online at any time.'

She's also working with another Lebanese friend, and fellow Parsons alumna, to launch a for-profit brand by the name of Second .ST.

'It's a new business model', she says. 'Second .ST pays half the rent and half the salaries, and 30 per cent of the profits go back into the brand. We think if we can actually build this brand, then we may be able to hire students to work with us after they graduate. Because the big question is always what happens next? We're a three-year programme, and there are very few jobs in fashion these days – and far fewer that pay well. So we want to be able to give CBS students a head start.'

Should that business model yields success, Sarah and Caroline have their sights set on an even grander goal: 'to start other free programmes in design, not only in fashion', she says. 'We believe that education should be accessible to everyone – not just the people who can afford it.' That's especially important, she adds, when it comes to design 'because designing your communities is an aspect of living, and too many people are left out of that process.'

To me, Sarah's story speaks volumes about the Arab world today – about the opportunities available to a select few and the deep reservoirs of talent that have for so long gone untapped. It is a story of steady, unyielding effort and hard-won success. But most of all, it's a story of possibility – of what can be achieved when we put aside our differences and come together. What Sarah and her supporters have built in Creative Space Beirut is more than a free fashion school, more than a brand. It's a template for progress.

Soraya Salti
Injaz al-Arab

LEARNING TO LEAD

IN THE FALL OF 2005, I CAME ACROSS A NEWSPAPER article about a Jordanian non-profit organisation by the name of Injaz Al-Arab. The article described how Injaz (Arabic for 'achievement') works to mobilise the private sector to prepare young people for careers in the global economy, primarily by recruiting corporate volunteers to go into schools and teach students about entrepreneurship.

Injaz had recently opened a chapter in Oman, and I knew then what a boon to our education system the organisation could be. What I didn't know was that the young woman behind it, a Jordanian entrepreneur by the name of Soraya Salti, would soon emerge as one of the most important voices in the Arab world. Over the next several years, I watched, as Salti turned a once floundering, cash-strapped initiative into one of the world's most influential NGOs, a feat for which she had received, in my opinion, far too little attention.

I decided then that I had to hear Salti's story in her own

words, and as she tells it, the road to success was largely unpaved when she started down it in the spring of 2001. Then a fledgling initiative, INJAZ had begun as a project of the aid group Save the Children, before being taken over by Junior Achievement Worldwide, the world's largest organisation dedicated to educating young people about entrepreneurship, financial literacy, and work readiness.

Junior Achievement needed an ambitious young leader to turn INJAZ around, and in many ways, Salti was a perfect fit for the job. She's bilingual in English and Arabic, holds undergraduate degrees in economics and accounting, and is a graduate of the distinguished executive M.B.A. programme at Northwestern University. During two years on the Innovative Competitiveness Team at Jordan's Ministry of Planning, Salti worked with renowned Harvard economist Michael Porter in furthering the country's economic development. Through previous stints at the Jordan–U.S. Business Partnership, the United Nations Economic and Social Commission for Western Asia and the World Economic Forum Action Group, she'd gained important insights about leveraging the private sector to strengthen education.

Perhaps more important, though, were Salti's intangibles. She had courage. She had drive. She relished a challenge, and like her mother, who started the Jordanian chapter of Save the Children in 1984 and ran it for nearly a decade, Salti was passionate about empowering the Arab youth.

Here was an opportunity for Salti to pick up where her mother had left off – to build on that progress and to make her own mark. Yet, the truth was, for all of Salti's ability, for all of her wit and charm and poise, the new executive wasn't so sure she was right for the job. You would never know it from watching the woman she is today, from the boundless confidence she exudes in every speech or the unwavering optimism with which she talks about the future.

But, for a time, Soraya Salti was actually afraid she might fail.

Sure, she had studied management under the best in the business. But up to that point, she had only ever managed a pair of interns. What would she do with a staff of 40? Salti had no idea, and for a few difficult weeks, she doubted whether she really belonged. Perhaps, there had been a mistake, she thought. Maybe they had confused her with another candidate. Or maybe they had been desperate to fill the position. After all, when Salti arrived on the job, INJAZ was in a dismal state.

Two years after its launch as a Save the Children initiative, the programme was still struggling to get off the ground. Jordan's Ministry of Education had provided only tepid support, and most in the private sector loathed getting involved. 'We knocked on so many doors urging business leaders to volunteer', Salti recalls. But the response was almost always the same: education, they'd tell her, was the government's job – not theirs. 'It was one rejection after another.' As a result, the INJAZ staff had become demoralised, and Salti most of all. 'Every day I wanted to resign.'

Then one day, Salti decided she'd had enough. Frustrated and fed up, she gathered her belongings and walked out the door. She wasn't quitting – not yet. But she wanted to see for herself whether the model was actually working.

For several days, Salti toured the handful of public schools then participating in the programme, dropping in to watch the private sector volunteers as they imparted their wisdom to Jordan's youth. The schools themselves, she says, were as rundown as they had always been: dilapidated desks, broken lights, paint peeling from the walls. From the outside, things didn't look very good.

But upon closer inspection, Salti saw that something remarkable was happening within them.

In a country where rote learning had long been the norm, students at the schools were actually interacting with their educators. Rather than being drilled and tested on regurgitating facts, they were huddling with volunteers, learning about work in the real world and how to prepare for it. Just as importantly, they were learning about themselves, about their strengths and weaknesses, about their potential as individuals.

'A transformation had taken place', Salti recalls. 'Everywhere I went; students were full of excitement and enthusiasm.' It was then, she says, that she fell in love with the model. 'I decided not to quit after all.'

Those scenes of eager, enthusiastic students was all the evidence Salti needed that she should stay – that INJAZ was, in fact, onto something. But there was one moment in particular that spoke to her on a personal level. At the last school she visited, Salti says, the volunteer, a greying, bespectacled executive from a local bank, posed a kind of existential question to the class.

'He asked them, *Why are you here? Why are you sitting in this classroom?* And a little boy with large, thick glasses replied, *because I want to be confident.* The volunteer said, *what was that? I can't hear you.* And the boy said again, a bit louder this time, *because I want to be confident.* And the volunteer said, *I still can't hear you, what did you say?* And the boy stood up, and this time he shouted, he said: *BECAUSE I WANT TO BE CONFIDENT!!!* And I said to myself, *Yes! Yes! That is me!*'

For Salti, that brief exchange was an epiphany. Watching that timid little boy as he summoned the courage to speak aloud in front of his peers, Salti saw in him something of herself. 'I had always been the shiest person in the room', she says. 'Even in my executive M.B.A. programme, my professors told me, "You have to speak! You're going to flunk if you don't speak!"'

From that moment on, Salti understood why *she* was there, too – and why, for a reason that had never before occurred to her, she was just the person for the job. You see, until that moment, Salti believed that success was a matter of brains and talent, and to some extent, luck. But it was by recognising that weakness she shared with the students themselves, the self-doubt that had all but muzzled her as a student and that had nearly moved her to resign, that Salti was able to empathise with the people INZAJ aimed to help.

'I realised that to lead this organisation, I would have to speak for the silent majority, for the youth of the Arab world', she says. 'But in order to become *their* voice, I knew I would have to find my own. That was the skill *I* had to acquire, and I had to acquire it fast.'

Thus began the journey Salti has been on ever since, an ambitious mission to transform classroom education across the Arab world and to equip Arab youth with the knowledge, skills and self-confidence they need to become agents of change.

A MOVEMENT IS BORN

Nowhere is the need for that change more urgent than in the Arab world.

According to the International Monetary Fund, unemployment in the MENA region is the highest in the world, and the region's youth shoulder the bulk of that burden: the rate amongst young people aged 15–29 is approximately four times that of the MENA as a whole, with roughly one in four going jobless. Every year, that youth unemployment runs the region an estimated US $50 billion in direct opportunity costs.

That's a product, in part, of demographic trends; some 65 per cent of the population of the Arab world is under the age of 25, more than twice the rate of North America. As this 'youth bulge' grows larger, job creation remains stagnant, and economic activity is in decline. Not only is unemployment amongst youth in MENA the highest in the world, it's often long lasting, and it's this duration, say experts, that does the most to undermine the accumulation of human capital, one of the primary drivers of economic growth.

Education in its current state has done little to help. With its emphasis on rote memorisation, the typical school curriculum is largely unaligned with private sector needs. As a result, schools are churning out graduates unprepared to compete in the global marketplace, sending a constant stream of young men and women into a talent pool few companies are willing to tap. The World Bank estimates that in order to absorb that human capital, MENA countries will have to create 80 million new jobs by 2020.

It's a daunting prospect. But if education has proved a dead end for Arab youth, entrepreneurship has emerged as a promising way forward. 'The public sector isn't going to create these jobs; big companies aren't going to create these jobs', Fadi Ghandour, CEO of Jordan-based express courier Aramex and an INJAZ AL-ARAB board member, told

Newsweek in 2010. 'The stability and future of the region is going to depend on our teaching our young people how to go out and create companies.'

ENTER INJAZ.

What began in 1999 with just a handful of schools and only three corporate partners had become, by 2002, a national entity. Across Jordan, business leaders were sending staff into local high schools and universities. For an hour each week, those volunteers were sharing with students the practical knowledge they'd gained from experience, explaining financial concepts – how to run a budget, how the stock market works – and fielding questions about their careers.

That progress wouldn't have been possible without INJAZ's first and most vocal champion, Queen Rania of Jordan. A fervent supporter from the very start, the Queen had volunteered in classrooms and encouraged business leaders to do the same, urging them to see INJAZ as an investment in the country itself. With the Queen's help, INJAZ grew by leaps and bounds, mobilising more than 3,000 private sector volunteers from 170 corporations, and providing training in entrepreneurship to more than a third of the country's students.

Business by business, school by school, INJAZ was bridging the gap between the public and private sectors, paving the way for a new kind of partnership, an approach to problem solving few in Jordan, or anywhere in the Arab world, had ever seen. By instilling in business leaders an appreciation for the magnitude of the country's unemployment crisis, Salti and team had switched on a light, illuminating an issue vital to the country's growth and stability, and provided them with a mechanism for addressing it.

Indeed, more than a mere initiative, INJAZ had grown into a movement. It came at just the right time: In 2003, Jordan's King Abdullah II launched the so-called Education Reform for Knowledge Economy (ERFKE) programme. A 5-year, US $500-million undertaking funded in part by the World Bank to train teachers, build schools and overhaul classroom curricula in line with the present-day demands of Jordan's job market.

'Jordan was really the lighthouse of education reform in the Arab world', says Salti, noting that the then minister of education, a nuclear physicist named Khaled Tuqan, had been tapped by the King to carry out the reforms. Tuqan, she adds, knew well how important education is to the future of the country.

As INJAZ picked up momentum, Tuqan took notice, and in 2004, when Salti was ready to expand its reach beyond Jordan's borders, he introduced her to his counterparts across the region. 'He wrote a letter to every country, saying *from a brother to a brother, I highly recommend this programme*. That opened some very big doors.' Meanwhile, as Regional Ambassador of INJAZ, Queen Rania urged Arab first ladies to support the organisation in their own countries. She also launched INJAZ in Kuwait, where she grew up. 'So Jordan played a big role', says Salti. 'It blazed the path we've taken to get to where we are today.'

Today, INJAZ Al-Arab reaches close to 2 million youths in 15 countries; counts amongst its 1,500 private sector partners the likes of MasterCard, ExxonMobil, Boeing and other Fortune 500s; and has introduced more than 10,000 corporate volunteers into more than 2,000 public schools across the Arab world.

Harder to quantify, but no less important, says Salti, is the change in mindset taking root throughout the region – both in boardrooms and in classrooms. Where youth have long aspired to join government jobs, says Salti, INJAZ is helping them envision a different future – to see their individual potential as entrepreneurs and job creators. Where corporate executives once dismissed the idea that the private sector should support education, more and more are seeing it as an investment and embracing opportunities to get involved.

INJAZ's spectacular rise earned it a place in *The Global Journal's* 2012 ranking of the Top 100 NGOs, putting it in the rare company of organisations like Oxfam, TED Talks, the Wikimedia Foundation and the Nobel Prize-winning Doctors Without Borders. It also brought Salti well-deserved praise for her visionary leadership, her efforts to challenge the status quo and to give the voiceless a voice. In 2006, she was named the Schwab Social Entrepreneur of the Year by the World Economic Forum. In 2009, she won the Skoll Award for Social Entrepreneurship, becoming the first Arab woman to win the honour and the US$1.25 million 'core support investment' that comes with it. In 2012, she added to her list of laurels the Henry R. Kravis Prize given out annually for 'extraordinary leadership in the non-profit sector.'

For Salti, though, no award could be as gratifying as seeing the student companies that emerge from the annual INJAZ Young Arab Entrepreneurs Competition. Designed to develop students' skills and showcase their creativity, the competition pits student teams from across the Arab world

– winners of their respective national competitions – against one another, in a duel for five prizes. After undergoing every step of building a company – forming a board, raising capital, developing a business plan and a marketing strategy, and producing and selling their products and services – the teams make their pitch to a panel of executives drawn from leading corporations around the world. Each year, one company comes away with the top prize, and more often than not, says Salti, the winners are girls.

'If you think that's by design, it isn't', she told an audience at Zayed University in the United Arab Emirates. 'It's by ambition, by skill, by leadership. These female teams want to demonstrate to their countries and to their peers that they are serious, that they have a new mindset that this region has never seen.' Seeing them succeed, she said, only strengthened her conviction that 'the future of the Arab world and the solutions that our region needs so desperately will be coming from these emerging young leaders.'

ONE MILLION AND COUNTING

Nicholas Kristof, the *New York Times* columnist and author, was covering the 2008 World Economic Forum in Davos, Switzerland when he received an invitation to a private audience with Queen Rania of Jordan.

The occasion was the launch by the Queen of INJAZ Al-Arab's 'One Million Arab Youth Campaign', an ambitious effort to empower one million students each year by 2018. Salti, who had been invited to Davos upon winning the Schwab Entrepreneur of the Year award, had reached out to fifty top business leaders, requesting their attendance at the exclusive event.

Before long, word had spread throughout town, and somehow, amid the high-octane networking of the global power elite, where the din of capitalism can drown out even the loudest of billionaire investors, a young woman few had ever heard of was making the most noise of all. Kristof had to know: Who was this Soraya Salti? And what exactly was INJAZ?

The two became good friends, and for Kristof, a Pulitzer-Prize winning journalist who has devoted his career to defending the downtrodden, particularly girls and women in the developing world, INJAZ has become a source of inspiration. In a column he penned later that week, he called the world's attention to its work, noting that 'girls in particular have flourished', and posited that 'Ms Salti will contribute more to the stability and peace in the Middle East than any number of tanks in Iraq, U.N. resolutions or summit meetings.'

Two years later, Kristof echoed that assessment in a column, celebrating the rise of entrepreneurship in Oman. Struck by how dramatically the country's investment in education had transformed the role of Omani women, he recounted meeting the finalists in Oman's Young Entrepreneurs Competition, almost all of whom were girls. One of them, an 18-year-old university student named Rihab, was a perfect example of how much had changed in just two generations: her grandmother, who is illiterate, was married at the age 9 and gave birth to 10 children. Rihab, however, had no plans to marry anytime soon; a husband, she mused, might weigh her down and keep her from pursuing her dreams, wherever in the world they might take her.

Rihab's concerns reflect the reality on the ground. A 2011 report by Booze & Co. on youth unemployment found that 'a mix of local norms and traditions, social beliefs and principles emanating from the G.C.C.'s patriarchal systems still, to some extent, exert an influence on young women's lives, limiting their opportunities.' Asked what role women should have in society, nearly 60 per cent of men who participated in the survey said women should be wives and mothers first. Yet more than 70 per cent of the women surveyed cited financial independence as their number one priority for seeking employment.

'There's a big gap between the aspirations, dreams and ambitions of females in this region and the perception by males of who they are and where they should be', says Salti. Yet, she said, another finding from the G.C.C. offered a measure of hope. 'In several regional markets, women are more highly educated than the general population, and by bringing more women into the workforce, companies can gain a competitive advantage.'

What's clear, she says, is that if the public sector was once a haven for female employment, those jobs are no longer there. As INJAZ aims to demonstrate, and as many women are beginning to see, the path forward will be through entrepreneurship, 'where only they are responsible for their economic destiny.'

To get where she is today, Soraya Salti had to shed the self-doubt that had for so long held her back. Only by finding her own voice was she able to speak for the people Injaz had set out to help – the many Arab youth ill-prepared for the white-collar jobs to which they aspire. Having done so, she's managed to transform INJAZ into a potent engine of entrepreneurship, sowing seeds of change in schools around the regionJust as important, she's come to serve as an example to young women everywhere.

Sultan Batterjee
A Developer with a Cause

SOME OF SULTAN BATTERJEE'S FONDEST MEMORIES TAKE him back to the dinner table at his childhood home in Jeddah, Saudi Arabia. There, his father and grandfather, both successful entrepreneurs, would sit for hours on end, discussing the finer points of a business plan or financing for a new project – and always with an eye, he recalls, to adding value to the community, to bettering Arab society at large.

'Their discussions were always so lively and intense', remembers Sultan, who as the owner and chief executive officer of the world-renowned design and construction company IHCC, as well as founder and president of Lifestyle Developers, has continued his family's legacy of business success in the fields of healthcare, pharmaceuticals, and education. Although much of what was said during those dinner table discussions was beyond the grasp of a young boy, it was there, he says, that the seeds of entrepreneurship and social responsibility were first sown. 'You might say they're part of my DNA.'

Indeed, as much as any trait Sultan inherited from his forebears, that familial wisdom passed down during his youth shaped his outlook on life and career, and propelled him forward. It was one thing, he understood, to generate profits. But to be the kind of executive he aspired to be, to leverage corporate success for social good, he would have to do much more. Poised to make his mark on the MENA region, and to carry on a family tradition of excellence in bringing to it innovative products and services, Sultan spent years in rigorous preparation, learning how to motivate and to manage – and above all, how to lead.

After high school in Saudi Arabia, Sultan went on to study abroad in the U.S. and U.K. He then cut his teeth in investment banking at several industry-leading firms – groups like Lazard Investments, Merrill Lynch, and Encore Management. In addition to providing him with much-needed structure, those experiences exposed him to the highest business standards and best practices on the planet, and when he returned to Saudi Arabia, Sultan hit the ground running. Eager to find opportunities for economic growth, he was also primed to have an impact on Saudi society, and as any observer of his companies can attest, the young developer has done just that.

Plenty of entrepreneurs can point to some way by which their work supports the local community. But a successful business built on giving back – well, that's something all too rare in today's Middle East. This is why, when I learnt of Sultan through an article in Forbes Middle East – 'Leaders Inspiring a Kingdom', a roundup of Saudi Arabia's entrepreneurial elite – I knew this book wouldn't be complete without his story. Forbes had ranked Sultan No. 1 in the field of real estate and construction, describing IHCC as 'perhaps best known for its network of Saudi German Hospitals.' Sultan himself, the article added, 'is currently working toward his master's in entrepreneurship at the renowned Massachusetts Institute of Technology (MIT).'

But Forbes, I later found, had barely scratched the surface. As I would learn through long conversations with Sultan himself, the Saudi national's rise to the top of Middle East real estate has had as much to do with the values that guide his companies' decision making as it has with the knowledge and skills he has acquired at places like M.I.T.

After all, he says, a company's values are fundamental to what it does. While people often talk about values, he says, few actually adhere to the ones they advertise. 'You can visit companies anywhere in the world, and you'll find that they have a set of values – sometimes as many as a dozen. But if you ask the employees what those values are, they usually can't name more than two or three.' Citing a global Delphi study published last year, Sultan notes that companies that can anchor just four values have a better working atmosphere and achieve a greater return on investment than those with more.

But just as important as the number, he says, is the role they play. 'Your values aren't a marketing tool. They aren't about telling the world how great you are.' Rather, he says, it's by identifying one's values that a company moulds its culture – the characteristics that define it. In order to do that, the company has to have a purpose.

Purpose. 'It's something higher than making money', says Sultan. 'Something you strive for. The CEO isn't just speaking off the cuff; a diligent student of management, he's researched the field extensively. 'And I've found that the companies that are successful today, the Microsofts and the Apples and the General Electrics and the Johnson & Johnsons – they share this in common; they have a higher purpose that makes the people who work for them want to get up in the morning and go to the office.'

A similar sense of purpose has long driven the young Saudi himself. Born into a wealthy family, Sultan need never have worried about earning a living; employment was always optional. 'I'm fortunate to have a father like mine', he says. 'I could have stayed home, done a few deals now and then, and relaxed. But that just isn't me. Ever since I was a kid, I've had this burning desire to do something big – something meaningful.'

Of course, Sultan's ascent didn't happen overnight. 'It's not that I just decided to become a developer, and I became a developer', he says with a laugh. 'It's been a journey.' Even before he knew what he wanted to do, Sultan had reached a certain conclusion about life, he says: 'I realised that you only go through it once, so you might as well do it to the fullest. Only then can you reap the rewards in the life after.' He also realised, he says, that every person should have a purpose too. 'And mine is to be a developer with a cause – to use my talents to build a sustainable future for my generation and for generations to come through the businesses that I run.'

CHANGING THE EQUATION

Stretching from Casablanca to Karachi, the MENA region is characterised by striking diversity – religious, ethnic, cultural, and more. But one characteristic is common throughout: an unprecedented, and ever growing, youth bulge'. According to the World Bank, an estimated 30 per cent of the MENA population is between the ages of 15 and 29, representing some 100 million youth. This marks the highest proportion of youths to adults in the region's history, a demographic shift with potentially dire implications for political stability and economic development.

For countries across the region, the choice is clear: invest in your young people, boys and girls, or suffer the consequences of inaction. Left to languish without proper education or the hope of gainful employment, the youth of the Arab world will only be a burden on development, and countries will have squandered the human capital so critical to their future growth. Saudi Arabia, as Sultan well knows, is no exception.

You know, they say we're rich in natural resources like oil and gas', he says. 'And I tell them, yes, that's true, but we have natural resources that are much more valuable than oil and gas; we have people. 70 per cent of the Saudi population is under the age of 30. That is a lot of young people.' Then he discovered another startling statistic, he says: '65 per cent of the people in Saudi Arabia don't own homes, and it's the same story in countries across the region. You're talking about tens of millions of people, many of whom are professionals contributing to the economy – engineers, doctors, bankers, lawyers – but the economy isn't giving nearly as much back to them.'

As the CEO of the award-winning design-and-build company IHCC, Sultan had long ago made a name for himself as a visionary leader. First launched as a spin-off from a larger firm, IHCC quickly emerged as a major player in Middle East real estate, winning numerous accolades for its world-class work designing, building and staffing large medical and educational facilities. Past projects run the gamut from hospitals and clinics to diagnostic centres, medical universities, libraries, and more in Saudi Arabia, the United Arab Emirates, and Egypt.

A $100-million, 300-bed hospital and housing project, designed and built by IHCC for the Middle East Health Care Company, won the award for ;Best Health Care Project' at the Saudi Arabian Building & Infrastructure Summit in 2011. At the 2nd annual Arab Investment Summit held in Abu Dhabi later that year, IHCC was recognised for its contributions to the development of Saudi Arabia's wellness sector with the award for 'Best Leisure Development Project'. Year after year, project after project, IHCC continued its steady ascent, cementing its reputation for excellence in delivering turnkey services.

It wasn't until he was married, though, that Sultan saw the potential for a company that could raise the standard of living across the region. 'After I got married, I needed to buy a house', he recalls. 'And when I started shopping for one, I was struck by how overvalued all of the properties were.' The rental market was no better: 'Nothing was designed to my taste, the quality of the construction wasn't very good, and everything was very costly', he says.

'And that's when I decided I would do something – something in the real estate field.'

Reflecting on his purpose – to be a developer with a cause – Sultan had a kind of epiphany; 'I thought to myself, I'm a young man, I'm educated and I'm capable. And God has chosen me to know things about design and construction. So, if I say I'm working with this purpose, then I should use that knowledge that God has given me to raise standards of living across the region – to change the equation.'

Thus was born Lifestyle Developers, a real estate development company, devoted as the name suggests, to enhancing people's quality of life. Sultan had decided that given the crowded competition for high net worth individuals and the government's focus on housing for low-income populations, he would target those in the middle – people whose needs he understood, whose tastes he could cater to. 'They want to be proud about where they live', he says. 'They want their home to reflect who they are. But they're not looking for the house of their dreams.'

These young professionals, he realised, men and women working hard to reach the next level, to move up in the corporate world, had been wasting their money. They would rent an overpriced apartment for five or ten years, and then they would move out. 'And when they did', he says, 'they owned nothing'. Sultan sought to offer these young professionals, 'the engines powering our growth', a dignified alternative. Rather than handing over their hard-earned income to a landlord who couldn't be bothered to fix a leaky faucet, they could spend the same amount to finance, and ultimately own a stylishly designed space in a Lifestyle Development building. 'After 10 years, they have the option to resell that or to rent it out to someone else, giving them a steady source of income.'

Every Lifestyle Developers project embodies four core elements: design, quality, affordability, and community. In addition to elegant décor and a full range of modern appliances, all apartments come with a long list of amenities, including shared spaces where neighbours can interact: a gym, a library, a nursery, indoor and outdoor gardens – even a ballroom. A concierge is on-call 24 hours a day, while CCTV cameras provide an extra layer of security. 'When they move in, residents receive a gift box explaining the whole concept', says Sultan. 'How to get in and out, how to treat one's neighbours, how to be part of a vibrant community.'

'We thought about the apartment as though we were building it for ourselves', he says. In fact, some employees of Lifestyle Developers have purchased units in the company's properties, reflecting 'our belief, our confidence in the product.'

TRUE GLOBALISATION

The continuous pursuit of knowledge: This, Sultan says, is the way of success, and it has taken him far and wide. 'I've learned a lot in my life from travelling', he says. 'From seeing other people develop different things with different ideas. I truly believe that every decision you make is informed by what you have seen – that it's a reflection of your experiences. While a person may naturally be very creative, he or she is limited by what they've been exposed to.'

That's one reason why Sultan takes time during every business trip to explore his surroundings, taking notes as he goes. 'When we're done with meetings for the day, I always try to get out and see as much of the city as I can, and particularly those areas that from a design standpoint are most aesthetically interesting or innovative.' It broadens his horizons, he says, and as a real estate developer, that's very important: 'to be able to think outside the box and to imagine news ways of doing things.' On a recent trip to Italy, for example – for the Milan International Furniture Fair – Sultan spent most of his time doing business. But he also had the opportunity to take in the neoclassical architecture, the buildings and boulevards, the piazzas and the parks.

'You see so many things that, at the time, your mind may not fully comprehend. But when you get back home, you start digesting those experiences, and I think they inform the way you approach your work. I always say, ideas don't come from the moon. They don't just fall in your lap. Ideas are created from other ideas, and from adapting those ideas to your own context.'

No less important, of course, is the education he's received at some of the world's most elite institutions. A graduate of Regent's Business School in London, Sultan went on to study strategic management at Oxford University before earning an Executive MBA at the American Management Association. After a number of years in the working world, Sultan resumed his studies at Harvard Business School, where he earned certificates in real estate finance and real estate development. He's now enrolled in a prestigious two-year master's programme in entrepreneurship at M.I.T.

While he's benefited from the intensive classroom instruction, just as valuable, he says, is the company of his peers. 'The more you surround yourself with successful people, the more likely you are to be successful', he says. 'Their attitudes, their ability to think critically and solve problems; that rubs on you. I've always found that, as a rule, successful people are eager to teach others what they've learned along the way. You just have to be willing to ask for their help – you can't be shy.'

That exposure to different people and places taught Sultan something else. Across the world, he says, standards are rising, and fast. 'In all the high streets, in all the cities across the globe, you see the same brands. And that's because 'globalisation' only really happened four years ago.' While air travel and international trade made the world a more connected place, true globalisation only came about with social media. 'Take a girl in a village in Egypt', he says. 'Seven years ago, if she bought a new bag, she would have compared herself to the other girls in her village; her standard would have been capped by her village.' Now she has Facebook, he says, 'and with a single click, she can compare herself to a girl in Miami Beach.'

The same applies to residential real estate. 'These young people aren't going to settle for just anything', he says. 'And that's why we're in this business of affordable luxury; we want them to be inspired by where they live, and we want them to stay here.' Like countries throughout the region, Saudi Arabia suffers from a brain drain – a loss of homegrown expertise and technical skill to other, more developed parts of the world.

'These young professionals get scholarships to study abroad in the U.S. or the U.K., and they become accustomed to a certain lifestyle.' Yet, when they return to the region, he says, they're not finding that lifestyle, so they decide to go back. 'And that's our loss – we lose these minds that the government and private sector have spent huge sums of money to educate and train.' Through projects like its new Diyar Al-Salam, or 'Homes of Peace' – 114 smartly-appointed apartments in the heart of Jeddah – Lifestyle Developers hopes to stem that trend.

"'We're a profitable business', says Sultan, 'but a lot of what we do goes back to the community and to helping ensure a sustainable future.' Whether it's building a library for an all-girls' school in Jeddah or carving out a rare green space for the general public, Lifestyle Developers often does pro-bono what the state can't or won't. 'There was an empty parcel of land in the desert that the Jeddah municipality had set aside to be a park', he recalls of the latter. 'But we knew how long that could take. So we decided to do it ourselves – to establish this park as a kind of example to other funds, other high net worth individuals.' Sultan named the park after himself not to boost his own ego, he says, but to make a point.

'I could have called the park anything. But I wanted to say to those high net worth individuals: Look, this young entrepreneur, this guy who is new in the game, is doing something for the public good. Your companies are worth billions. So if I can do this, just imagine what you could do. I'm not saying everyone should build a park – there are many other things that could benefit the community. But if these big players were to put aside just a small amount of money every year for the youth – for that 70 per cent of the population – we would have green cities in no time. We would have a very different region.'

More than a green space, Sultan Batterjee Park stands as a testament to the power of purpose and the work of a visionary. Indeed, through his continuous pursuit of knowledge, and an inexhaustible resolve to raise standards of living across the region, Sultan has come to serve as a model of success – an inspirational figure, not only to his peers in the industry, but to the unsung millions across the Arab world with ambitions of becoming a successful entrepreneur.

Tariq al-Barwani
Knowledge Oman

Information technology and communications have now become the main elements that move forward the development process in this third millennium: therefore, we have accorded our attention to finding a national strategy to develop the skills and abilities of citizens in this domain.

        – Sultan Qaboos bin Said al Said

IN HIS ADDRESS AT THE OPENING SESSION OF THE COUNCIL of Oman, the country's bicameral parliament, in November, 2008, His Majesty Sultan Qaboos instructed the government to act with speed in implementing the Digital Oman Strategy, an e-governance initiative designed to leverage information technology for social and economic gain.

A blueprint for key IT initiatives, aimed at empowering citizens and improving public services, was only the latest iteration of a modernisation campaign which began decades ago. Indeed, from the day he assumed power in July, 1970, paving the way for the Renaissance that would make Oman a paragon of enlightened leadership, Sultan Qaboos has pinned the country's economic hopes not on its finite supplies of crude oil, but on a far more valuable, and sustainable, resource: the Omani people.

To that end, His Majesty made education a national priority, using the country's newly discovered oil reserves to bankroll its future: hundreds of new schools and salaries for thousands of new teachers. In 1970, fewer than 300 students were enrolled in the country's three schools. Today, Oman boasts more than 1,200 schools, employing more than 40,000 teachers, a range of public and private universities, and free education for all citizens, boys and girls alike.

It was this vision for Oman's future, His Majesty's master plan for transforming the Sultanate into a knowledge-based society that inspired Tariq al-Barwani to establish the country's first online portal for sharing knowledge. Widely known as 'Oman's popular IT expert', Tariq has long sought to harness his passion for technology for the benefit of Omani society, and Knowledge Oman, his innovative, award-winning project, does just that, bringing together professionals from across a spectrum of industries – both expats and locals – to exchange expertise and generate new ideas.

Tariq's creation has connected Omanis and expats living in Oman in a way we never were before. Which is why, when I considered candidates for this book, the young tech guru, with his magnetic personality and immeasurable impact, came immediately to mind. More than a successful entrepreneur – and that he is – Tariq has used his skill-set to give back to the community and to help others succeed. Through Knowledge Oman, he and his team have identified talented individuals worthy of wider recognition, and leveraged the power of the Internet to amplify their voices, educating and inspiring young people across the country.

'We started as a simple forum', he told me recently, recalling the time in 2008 when Knowledge Oman was first getting off the ground. 'Then we started offering seminars, and then we built a knowledge sharing platform specifically engineered to develop the information and communication technology sector in Oman. And now everything we do, we do as volunteers.'

In the seven years since, Knowledge Oman has grown by leaps and bounds. The non-profit organisation currently boasts a variety of projects, including its 'KO Ambassadors' initiative, which enlists knowledge ambassadors, experts in their respective fields, to deliver free talks and workshops at colleges around the country. There's also the annual 'Knowledge Summit', which aims to bring Omani youth under one roof, "to learn and grow and get inspired," while 'KO Community Seminars' facilitate learning and networking amongst professionals, and the list goes on.

'Every day is a new day', Tariq said with characteristic optimism, grinning as he so often does, and with good reason. A much sought-after speaker, he's given numerous talks at universities, companies, events, and other forums. 'For those of you who don't know me', he told a TEDx audience in Muscat last year, 'my name is Tariq al-Barwani, and I'm your new friend.' Pacing the stage in a brown dishdasha, he delivered an energetic sermon on the keys to creating a winning organisation, punctuating each point with an emphatic finger in the air. 'Success, ladies and gentleman, is all about passion', he said. 'And do not underestimate the power of people.'

People, he went on, are the backbone of a successful organization – its strongest asset, the driving force behind its work. Attracting talented and passionate people, and promoting their work, is precisely how Knowledge Oman came to be the force for good it is today. 'We are an organisation made of people, by people, and for the people', he said. As we're living in a knowledge age, he added, 'We at Knowledge Oman would like to encourage innovation and to build a community.' That, in turn, he added, would generate 'a thriving economy.'

Paradoxically, Knowledge Oman's success has come in a large part by giving back. In collaboration with the Information Technology Authority and Microsoft Inc., the organisation has helped dozens of Omanis obtain certification as IT professionals. The group has also partnered with the largest electronics store in Oman to educate customers on IT products. Through donations of educational materials and visits to colleges and universities, Tariq and team have helped students and faculty members navigate the often bewildering landscape of IT technologies and associated career opportunities.

'We've worked with the U.S. Embassy in Muscat to empower Omani youth', he says. With the establishment of the 'Microsoft App Academy', Knowledge Oman now teaches people of all ages how to develop applications using their smart phones, tablets or personal computers. Recent years have also seen the launch of SmartWoman, a mobile platform designed to promote networking amongst Omani women and to help women learn from one another's experiences using customised local content. A first-of-its-kind initiative in the country, SmartWoman was rolled out in collaboration with KO's telecom partner Ooreedoo, and supported by Qualcomm® Wireless Reach™.

Another first for the Sultanate was the Knowledge Oman e-School. The country's first free e-learning platform, the

KO e-School offered ICT courses to hundreds of young Omanis in both English and Arabic, representing a major step forward for free online education in the country, and with 'OmanVideos.com', Knowledge Oman introduced the Sultanate's first bilingual video sharing platform. Aimed at nurturing creativity, the site allowed visitors from anywhere in the world to register, view, and easily upload videos.

Some of those projects have since come to an end, says Tariq. But with 15,000 members and counting, KO continues to grow.

COMING OF AGE

Tariq Hilal Al-Barwani was born in Muscat in 1979. It was his father, he says, Hilal Masoud al-Barwani, who introduced him at the age of 5 to his first computer – 'the ZX Spectrum!' he recalls with a chuckle – igniting his passion for the revolutionary new machine. It was also his father, he says, who instilled in him the love for learning that has fuelled his career ever since. 'He's really been the cornerstone of my success', Tariq told me, describing his father, who before his retirement was for many years a banker, as both a 'personal mentor' and a 'close friend.'

'My dad showed me that the computer was more than just about playing games – that I could use it to affect change', he says. 'To create things which help other people.' From his father, he says, he learned that by helping others, Tariq could help himself. 'And that, I think, is the best way to be successful', he says. 'It's not the only way. But if you can work with other people, if you can help them find their strengths, if you can help them reach their potential – that way, *believe me*, the sky is the limit. That, he says, is what

Knowledge Oman is all about. 'Everyone here is a winner because we help one another win.'

Of course, Tariq was also enamored with the technology itself. 'Usually, people like to play games, and to move from one level to another', he says, reminiscing about his earliest engagement with computers. 'But for myself, I always wanted to be *inside* the game – to really understand *how* you move from one level to another.' Indeed, more than a source of amusement or entertainment, the computer was, for Tariq, a strange world to be explored – a mystery to be unraveled and understood; and that he did. A curious and a very precocious boy, Tariq immersed himself in the study of programming.

At the age of 13, Tariq was selected to join the Omani Science Club, and travelled to Bahrain to represent Oman regionally. It wouldn't be long before he was off to Novia Scotia in eastern Canada to pursue a bachelor's degree in Information Systems and Computer Science at Acadia University. Over his fours year at Acadia, Tariq excelled in the classroom, developing as a programmer and eventually graduating with honours – a standout student with a bright future in the field.

'My first job was with a fantastic company called United Media Services', he recalls. 'We were the first in Oman to coin the word "portal", which is a website designed to serve as a web user's homepage and as a directory for finding information.' In 1999, Tariq singlehandedly developed the Sultanate's first IT portal. Dubbed Tariq.net, the portal delivered the latest news on the IT scene, both in Oman and abroad, through a variety of offerings, including information on jobs, conferences, free downloads, and more. Within just three months of its launch, Tariq.net was acquired by

Oman Holdings International (OHI), one of the largest holding groups in the country, and Tariq was brought on as an internet services manager.

It was a life-changing moment. Not only had his portal been purchased in a big-dollar deal; it was also voted the best website in Oman for the year 2000, sealing his reputation as one of the Sultanate's most important new voices. In his new job at OHI, Tariq hit the ground running; in addition to overseeing the management of the portal he'd created, he started up and staffed the organisation's Internet Development Department, which continues to serve clients to this day.

After two years at OHI, Tariq left to continue his studies, taking his place in a Master's programme in Information Technology at Swinburn University of Technology in Melbourne, Australia. Just as he did at Acadia, Tariq consistently outperformed his peers, becoming a student of distinction and a source of advice to his fellow classmates. Moreover, in addition to honing his technical skills and strengthening his grasp of IT's complexities, Tariq also took professional courses in business and management – a 'mini MBA' – equipping himself with the knowledge he needed to one day go out on his own.

Armed with a graduate degree, Tariq took a job as an online manager at Nawras (now Ooredoo Oman), the Sultanate's first privately owned telecommunications companyThere, as everywhere, he shined. In charge of managing and coordinating the company's day-to-day online operations, and building the Nawras brand, Tariq also designed the company's intranet, a computer network used for sharing information within an organisation. He also designed its external website, which went on to win local and international web awards. In time, Tariq moved up the ranks at Nawras, becoming the head of corporate affairs, where he oversaw public relations, marketing, and media relations.

Still, what made Tariq tick and made him get up in the morning and go to work, wasn't the title or the influence or the size of his paycheck. Rather, it was the prospect of helping people – of bettering his country by sharing his knowledge with as many people as he could.

After all, for years, Tariq had been penning weekly columns for two of the country's largest newspapers, the Times of Oman and Al Watan, on issues related to information and communications technology. Through those columns – known as 'Tariq Online' – he aimed to improve digital literacy amongst Omani youth, readying them for a job market where digital skills are increasingly in demand. In this endeavour too, Tariq had blazed a new trail, becoming the first columnist in Oman to write articles on IT in both languages, thereby maximising the medium's reach.

Later, he had the idea to broadcast that message through different media. 'I went to the Ministry of Information, and I said, hey, why don't we create a programme that would spread awareness about IT in Oman', he recalls. 'So, we introduced "Raqmyaat", the first TV show, and "CyberTalk", the first FM programme on IT.' Over the following three years, Tariq wrote, edited, and hosted the weekly programmes – 'everything from concept to execution', he says. The programmes covered the latest local and international IT news, product reviews, tips and tricks, and featured interviews with guests, typically experts on a given topic, as well as a question and answer session with audience members. Both programmes continue today by other presenters.

For all of his notoriety, though, Tariq had always been inclined to altruism. As a child, he was using computers to perform automated tasks for the members of his family. Later, he started creating applications, including one to counter the viruses that were, at the time, penetrating many people's computers; wiping out hard drives and robbing users of their intellectual property. 'So, I developed a kind of software that could clear people's computers of these viruses', he recalls. 'And then I placed that software online for anyone to download for free.'

In 1999, after the government-owned General Telecommunications Organisation (GTO) was privatised, the new Oman Telecommunications Company encountered a problem: all of its subscribers were stuck with Internet settings using the web address for the GTO. Tariq had an idea. 'I said, why don't I create for you a programme that can transfer your entire user base from the old site to the new one?', he recalled.

With a few clicks, the programme, dubbed GTO-2-Omantel, would automatically reconfigure subscribers' Internet settings, allowing some 20,000 people to be simultaneously converted to the new site. Several weeks later, the programme went public, and Omantel executives were ecstatic. Thanks to Tariq's handiwork, a potentially costly problem was quickly and easily averted.

WINNING

From the day he started down this road, Tariq has had to overcome obstacles, big and small. 'I've overcome a lot of challenges', he tells me. 'Whenever you talk about ideas with people, things that have never been done before, you get a number of people who tell you one of two things: either that your idea is not a good one or that it can't be done – that you're dreaming.' Time and again, Tariq proved his doubters wrong. 'I would always say to myself, no, it *is* possible. And I kept going and pushing ahead.'

'It may sound cliché', he adds, flashing that signature grin. 'But I believe I've gotten to where I am today because I've lived by a simple motto: if there is a will, there is a way.' He repeats the phrase like a mantra: *If there is a will, there is a way.* 'It's true. I've always kept that in my mind. And then, once you've achieved that thing you're going for, you search for something else – the next big project.'

That ceaseless search for something else has met with repeated success, bringing Tariq well-deserved recognition from around the world – and even a measure of fame. His various awards and distinctions are too many to list, but to name just a few: there was the Best Personality Award from Oman's Telecommunication Regulatory Authority; the Creative Man of the Year award he received at the 2012 Asian Leadership Conference in Seoul, South Korea; and an award from the Indian Ambassador to Oman for his contributions to the IT sector in 2013. Tariq also received the Visionary Leadership Award in 2014 at the Knowledge Management Summit 2014 in Banglore.

Most impressive, though, would have to be the Microsoft Most Valuable Professional (MVP) Awards. In recognition of his efforts to support Oman's technical and community initiatives, Microsoft, the largest software company in the world, has bestowed upon Tariq its MVP Award a staggering 9 years in a row. In Oman, only one person amongst hundreds from both the public and private sectors has been awarded the Microsoft MVP consecutively so many times. 'MVPs represent technology's best and brightest, who share a deep commitment to community and a willingness to help others', Microsoft Corporate Vice President Rich Kaplan said upon awarding Tariq his fifth MVP in 2011. 'We are honoured to welcome Tariq as one of them.'

KnowledgeOman.com has won its share as well – amongst them an International Standard Web Technology Award from the 2009 Oman Web Awards; a 2012 Strategic Cultural Award from the Pan Arab Web Awards; and an award for Outstanding Contribution to the Cause of Education presented at the 2012 World Human Resource Development Congress.

'I thought to myself, I've got these two hands', he told the TEDx audience in Muscat, holding them out as he recalled the moment in 2008 when the idea for Knowledge Oman first crystallised in his mind. 'What if I could have four hands? What if I could have a hundred hands? A thousand hands?' Over the past 10 years, he said, he'd gone from Muscat to Salala to build awareness about IT. He'd created TV and radio shows, written articles and given talks. But all of his efforts, he knew, could only accomplish so much. Because, after all, he was only one man.

How, Tariq wondered, could he continue that work on a larger scale. 'And I thought, instead of one person, let's do it by *many* people.' His voice grew louder, as the excitement of that moment, that realisation, came rushing back to him. 'It was the ability to touch and impact many people at the same time, speak one language and Share one message!' It was a labour of love, he explained. 'You don't get paid, but the opportunity to work with the most talented people in this country – now that is reward in itself. You get an opportunity to do things you normally cannot do in a paid job.' While one's successes as an employee are all about the employer, at Knowledge Oman, he said, 'it's all about you!'

A proud product of Oman, Tariq al Barwani leveraged the Internet's reach to empower his fellow countrymen. Drawing his inspiration from His Majesty, he set about building something the Sultanate had never seen – a tool that could amplify the country's professional expertise and help prepare young people for a future economy in which oil plays only a minor role. Never deterred by doubts, Tariq moved forward with the courage of his convictions – and in this, he's an example to us all.

Conclusion

THE ARAB WORLD, WE ARE OFTEN TOLD, IS A REGION IN turmoil – rife with corruption, mired in violence, plagued by weak institutions and the chronic poverty of its people.

To be sure, from Algiers to Aden, crises abound. None is more tragic or devastating than the conflict in Syria. Now in its fourth year, the war stands as one of the worst humanitarian disasters of our time, leaving, at last count, an estimated 200,000 dead and unleashing a refugee crisis of enormous proportions; so far, some four million Syrians have sought sanctuary abroad, putting unprecedented pressure on neighbouring countries to take them in and raising the prospect of a 'lost generation' of Syrian youth.

Meanwhile, in the absence of state authority, extremism flourishes, fueling unrest and fanning the flames of sectarian warfare. In Libya, in Yemen, and across Iraq, fighting rages on, as Egypt, the most populous country in the Arab world, stumbles toward an uncertain future, and the decades-long struggle between Israelis and Palestinians remains, as ever, at an impasse.

Such are the storylines that dominate coverage of the

region, and to the extent that the media shapes public perceptions of Arab society and the Middle East; this is clearly problematic. A focus on strife and suffering leaves little room for reporting on the issues and individuals that embody the vast potential of the Arab people. As a result, we are all too often reduced to a caricature, defined by our failings and misfortunes, and deprived of recognition for the many achievements, large and small, that go unseen.

It is my firm belief that this has to change – that if we are to one day overcome the deeply entrenched obstacles to a peaceful, prosperous Middle East, we must do more to counter the master narrative, to show our young people what is truly possible and to provide them with that most precious commodity: hope for a brighter future.

The individuals featured here are names only a few readers are likely to have heard before. No actors or athletes, no politicians or performers. None, as yet, a global celebrity. Rather, they are ordinary people – husbands and wives, brothers and sisters, sons and daughters. People, in other words, like you and me, and their stories – of bold risks and big rewards, of storms weathered and trails blazed, of toughness and resolve, courage and compassion – are as real as the paper they're printed on.

These stories are proof, too, that we need not look to ancient history for examples of the greatness of the Arab world. They are, in fact, all around us – independent, motivated young men and women who've refused to follow the flock, choosing instead to brave the unknown, to risk failure, and make mistakes in an effort to learn, to grow and, ultimately, to innovate. Pioneers and problem-solvers, they possess what Sultan Batterjee, founder and chief executive of the Saudi real estate firm Lifestyle Developers, describes simply as *purpose*. 'It's something higher than making money', he says. 'Something you strive for.'

Indeed, it's the good that comes of their work, the positive social impact, that at once fuels their ambition and sets them apart, making them, in my estimation, the 'stars' they are today. Sultan, as we've seen, is a prime example. The son of a successful developer, he need never have worried about his own financial wellbeing. But ever since he was a boy, he has had a burning desire, he says, 'to do something big, something meaningful.' That he has, becoming a 'developer with a cause', committed, as he puts it, to providing young professionals with a standard of living they've come to expect. This, he hopes, can help companies attract talent, and perhaps stem the brain drain that has long robbed the region of its best and brightest.

Tunisian financier-turned-philanthropist Lotfi Maktouf is equally mindful of the importance of investing in young people – and of the perils of neglecting to do so. Lotfi's rise from humble origins to Harvard Law School led to a lucrative job with a firm on Wall Street, and later to a senior position at the International Monetary Fund. From there, he might simply have coasted to a comfortable retirement. But like Sultan, Lotfi sought to do 'something meaningful', to give back, and in the wake of the anti-government protests that shook Tunisia in December 2010, kicking off what would come to be known as the Arab Spring, he leapt into action.

Almadanya, the non-political philanthropic organization Lotfi founded months later, targets the root causes of that unrest – namely, the underrepresentation of youth in the country's economy and the disenfranchisement of large segments of the population, particularly women.

Almadanya's programmes aim to expand access to quality education and vocational training, to fight school dropout and to increase female participation in the workforce, among other things. 'Our mission is to inspire Tunisians to dare', Lotfi explained. 'To begin the work today that will allow our youth to live a better tomorrow.'

Lotfi isn't alone in his efforts. Governments around the region are grappling with the same pressing question: how to help growing numbers of young people become productive members of society, participate in public life and reach the heights of their human potential. The challenge stems in large part from demographics; some 65 percent of the Arab world is below the age of 25, more than twice the rate of North America. Yet, as this 'youth bulge' continues to swell, stubbornly low job creation lags far behind, resulting in a youth unemployment rate of approximately 25 percent, the highest in the world.

Those statistics are powerfully illustrated in an infographic by Visualizing Impact, the Beirut-based organisation, co-founded by Joumana Jabri and Ramzi Jaber. Produced in partnership with Silatech, 'The Long Run' depicts the problem of youth unemployment worldwide, with a focus on age of independence. Nowhere, as it shows, do young men and women have to wait longer to acquire their first professional experience than in the MENA region, and that delay comes at a great cost – approximately $40–$50 billion annually. According to the U.N.'s International Labor Organization, if the region could achieve the global average of 13 percent unemployment, GDP could increase by $25 billion by 2018.

Joblessness in the MENA region is marked also by its duration, and it's this, say experts, that does the most to undermine the accumulation of human capital, one of the main forces propelling economic growth. Moreover, with few prospects for gainful employment, many young Arabs feel they have no stake in their nation's future. Hopeless and disengaged, they become a drag on growth, rather than a driver of it and, worse, ripe for recruitment by extremist elements who tend to prey on desperation and poverty.

It's now clear that this path simply isn't sustainable. MENA countries must do more to ensure that youth are equipped with the skills and social capital to not only survive in a global marketplace, but to prosper. For an even graver threat to the region than radicalism, I believe, is the danger that governments will fail to harness what is arguably their greatest asset – the raw talent, intellect, and creative energy coursing through their young populations. Such a failure would be catastrophic, both for the financial burden it would impose on governments already struggling to provide adequate social services, and for the destabilising effects of a deepening divide between the rich and poor.

We stand today at a precipice. Before us stands an unprecedented window of opportunity, a decade during which policymakers can take meaningful steps to promote inclusive economic growth, by fostering a more enabling environment for private enterprise, reducing the bloated public sector, rooting out corruption and, importantly, raising female participation in the labour force. On these and other measures, many countries have come quite far. But as the data indicate, there is still far to go.

Take, for example, a recent report on youth unemployment in the GCC by Booze & Co., which found that nearly 60 percent of men polled said women should be wives and mothers first. Yet, 70percent of women surveyed cited financial independence as their number one priority for seeking employment, revealing what the Jordanian entrepreneur Soraya Salti describes as a yawning gap 'between the aspirations, dreams and ambitions of females in this region and the perception by males of who they are and where they should be.'

It's an ironic fact that, across the Arab world today, women outnumber men in tertiary education. Young girls are less likely to enter school in the first place, but when they do, they tend to outperform boys and they matriculate to university in higher numbers. In the U.A.E., some 70 percent of university graduates are women, while in Qatar, nearly seven times as many women as men are enrolled in university, according to figures recently compiled by the World Bank. Over the past decade, almost all MENA countries closed the gender gap in education by at least 90 percent.

In spite of these gains in educational attainment, though, women are still far less likely than men to enter the job market. Three out of every four women remain outside the labour force. Of those women who do seek work, fewer than 44 percent find formal jobs, resulting in an unemployment rate roughly twice that of young men. Maysa Jalbout, a fellow at the Brookings Institution's Center for Universal Education, has termed this the 'boomerang effect', and the trend continues in countries throughout the region, nearly all of which remain well below the global average for female employment.

Education systems, too, are failing Arab youth, men and women alike. In many MENA countries, unemployment rates are in fact highest among the most educated segment of the youth population, indicating a mismatch between the skills students are learning at university and those in demand by the job market. With its emphasis on rote memorisation, the typical school curriculum does little to ready students for jobs in a knowledge economy. The result: a constant stream of young men and women into a talent pool few companies are willing to tap. The World Bank estimates that in order to absorb that human capital, MENA countries will have to create 80 million new jobs by 2020.

That's a formidable task for even the best performing economies. Governments, long being the largest employers in the region, can't do it themselves. Nor can the private sector, which hasn't expanded fast enough to keep pace with population growth.

But there is reason for hope. If education has proved a dead end for Arab youth, entrepreneurship has emerged as a promising way forward, a potential path out of the woods to a stable, self-sustaining future. Across the Arab world, a movement is underway to make young people the engines of a kind of economic awakening, a region-wide resurgence driven by creativity and innovation. From the Maghreb to the gulf, new programmes are sprouting up to teach students how to start their own companies, to become the job creators of tomorrow, and for years, Injaz al-Arab has been at the forefront of those efforts.

First launched in Jordan as an initiative of the aid group Save the Children, Injaz has been implementing educational programmes since 1999, providing students with training on entrepreneurship, financial literacy, and the soft skills that make them more employable. When Soraya took the reins of the organisation in 2001, Injaz was struggling to get off the ground. Jordan's Ministry of Education wasn't particularly interested in the idea, and corporations generally shied away from assisting with what they felt was the government's duty.

But Soraya had a vision for what Injaz could become, and she pursued it with a single-minded passion for giving 'a voice to the voiceless' – to the millions of Arab students made to sit silently in lifeless classrooms as teachers droned on, never inviting participation or encouraging debate. Soraya had her doubts. She wasn't sure, at first, that she was right for the job. But over the next several years, she managed to turn a cash-strapped initiative limited, at the time, to a few schools in Jordan into one of the world's most influential NGOs.

Today, Injaz reaches close to 2 million youths in 15 countries; counts among its 1,500 private sector partners the likes of MasterCard, ExxonMobil, Boeing and other Fortune 500s; and has sent some 10,000 corporate volunteers to equip students in more than 2,000 public schools with an entrepreneurial skill-set, relevant to the current labour market. As the New York Times columnist and author Nicholas Kristof wrote in a piece praising that work, 'Ms. Salti will contribute more to stability and peace in the Middle East than any number of tanks in Iraq, U.N. resolutions or summit meetings.' Anyone familiar with this remarkable leader would surely agree.

As we've seen from the stories collected here, to innovate is to take risks, and failure is a necessary part of the process. No matter how successful the organisation, every entrepreneur suffers setbacks. In fact, it's often said that those who've achieved greatness have failed greatly; the key is to keep going, to pick up the pieces, and carry on in the face of adversity. Or in the words of Safiya al-Bahlani, the Omani artist and graphic designer, to use 'challenge as your weapon'.

Few entrepreneurs have encountered the kind of challenges Safiya faced from the outset. Born with a congenital disorder called phocomelia, she has no forearms, a deformed knee, a deformed foot and is deaf in one ear. But by leaving her physically dependent, phocomelia had made her mentally tough, able to rise above the harsh insults hurled at her daily and to pursue her dream of becoming a painter. By the time she was a teenager, Safiya was so accustomed to confronting challenges that she began to seek them out. 'As an artist, I always looked for the hardest thing I could do', she says. 'And I always found a way. Nothing stopped me.'

For the Emirate animator Mohammed Harib, failure came in the form of a report card. As a freshman at Northeastern University in Boston, Massachusetts, Mohammed flunked his first class in architecture, and was kicked out of the programme. Forced to switch majors, he resisted pressure to study something more 'practical', and chose the general arts, which required him to take a course in animation. It was there, he says, that he first sketched 'Um Saeed', the foundational character for what would become the Middle East's first 3D animated TV series – the path-breaking and wildly popular show, FREEJ. 'How many times was I told, No?' He says. 'You have to believe in yourself. You have to have the courage to defend your ideas. And you have to be persistent.'

Raghda el-Ebrashi is persistence personified. Founder of the Cairo-based Alashanek Ya Balady (AYB), a social enterprise designed to create employment for marginalised youth, Raghda spent years learning from her friend and mentor, Om Fathi, before launching the first developmental student club at the American University of Cairo. At first, many of her fellow students disparaged the idea, and for a time Raghda wondered if anything would ever come of her efforts. But in time, others joined her cause, volunteering to teach underprivileged youth market-relevant skills, and thereby bridging the gap between the outputs of Egypt's failing education system and the vastly different demands of the labour market.

'It may sound cliché', says Omani IT expert Tariq al-Barwani, founder and president of Knowledge Oman, 'but I believe I've gotten to where I am today because I've lived by a simple motto: if there is a will, there is a way.' The country's first online portal for knowledge sharing, Knowledge Oman, evolved from a small forum into an award-winning organisation that has connected Omanis in a way we never were before. 'Whenever you talk about ideas with people, things that have never been done, people often tell you one of two things', he says. 'Either that your idea is not a good one or that it can't be done.' Time and again, Tariq has proved his doubters wrong. 'I would always say to myself, No, it *is* possible. And I kept going, kept pushing ahead.'

Fellow Omani Mutassem al-Sharji learned perseverance from the martial arts. Drawn to the structure and discipline of karate, he endured years of grueling training to become a black belt, and went on to co-found his own studio, The Strive Karate Club, in Muscat. Karate had also taught Mutassem to avoid the comfort so many people seek out, and it was with this in mind that he quit his job as an economist, pursuing instead, his lifelong passion for personal growth. A motivational speaker and writer, Mutassem launched the Enriching Experience, a social enterprise designed to promote learning through interpersonal exchange – an antidote to the anonymity of social media.

Before she founded the Creative Space Beirut, the Lebanese fashion designer Sarah Hermez had searched in vain for the perfect job, one that would allow her to combine her dual passions – creativity and social justice. But even after the free school for fashion design was up and running, the way forward was far from clear. 'I had never been a leader before', she recalled. 'I was very comfortable following people I respected, but I was never a mentor.' One after another, the challenges came, and as often as she failed, Sarah found a way to make things work – to offer underprivileged students access to an industry long reserved for the rich, and to break down walls between people of different backgrounds.

Together, these unseen stars represent, I believe, hope for our collective future. Men and women who have cut their own paths; who have, through sheer tenacity and force of will, turned their dreams into reality. They are living proofs that amid the maelstrom of violence and chaos engulfing much of the region, positive change is in the offing. It has been my privilege to record their stories, and it is my fervent hope that by broadcasting them across the Arab world, this book can serve to inspire young readers to reach higher, to dig deeper, and to discover the greatness that lies within us all.